SWU-700-006

UNIFORMS OF RUSSIAN ARMY OF PETER I THE GREAT

FROM THE REIGN OF PETER I TO CATHERINE II. PETER II, ANNA AND IVAN VI. 1682-1741

From the Viskovatov's greatest work:
"Historical description of the clothing and
arms of the Russian Army"

SOLDIERSHOP PUBLISHING

AUTHOR

Aleksandr Vasilevich Viskovatov born 22 April (4 May New Style) 1804, died 27 February (11 March) 1858 in St. Petersburg, Russian military historian. He graduated from the 1st Cadet Corps and served in the artillery, the hydrographic depot of the Naval Ministry, and then in the Department of Military Educational Institutions. He mainly studied historical artifacts and the histories of military units. Viskovatov's greatest work was the Historical Description of the Clothing and Arms of the Russian Army.

PUBLISHING'S NOTE

NOTE ABOUT BOOK PRINTING BEFORE 1925

LICENSES COMMONS

ACKNOWLEDGEMENTS

A Special Thanks to Boris Megorsky of the Re-Enactment Group "Preobrazhensky Life Guard Regiment, 1709» Saint – Petersburg, Russia and to NYPL and other institutions for their kindly permission to use some images of his archives, collections or books used in our book.

Title: **UNIFORMS OF RUSSIAN ARMY OF PETER I THE GREAT**
from the reign of Peter I to Catherine II, Peter II, Anna and Ivan VI - 1682-1741
By A.V.Viskovatov. Serie edit by Luca S. Cristini. First edition by Soldiershop. June 2017
Cover & Art Design: Luca S. Cristini. Plates re-colorations by Anna Cristini.
ISBN code: 978-88-93272506
Published by Soldiershop publishing, via Padre Davide, 7 - 24050 Zanica (BG) ITALY. www.soldiershop.com

UNIFORMS OF THE RUSSIAN ARMY OF PETER I THE GREAT

FROM THE REIGN OF PETER I TO CATHERINE II
PETER II, ANNA AND IVAN VI - 1682-1741

Peter Ist the Great of Russia 1672-1725 by Paul Delaroche (1838 C. Kunsthalle, Hamburg)

HISTORICAL DESCRIPTION OF THE CLOTHING AND ARMS
OF THE RUSSIAN ARMY - A.V. VISKOVATOV

Soldiershop is glad to presents the complete collection of the great job made by A.V. Viskovatov dedicated to the uniforms and weapons belonging from the first Zar and Russian emperors to the Russian army during the Napoleonic period, until 1860 about. The time we considered in this volume corresponds to the reigns of Catherine the Great (Catherine II) who reigned since 1762 until his murder on the 6 November 1796.

Our reprint in based on the original 19th century volumes, to be precise the volumes from 4 to 6 are dedicated to the reign of Catherine II; this part is distributed on 3 or 4 volumes.

Our new edition, the first ever published in English, both on paper and digital format, boasts a large number of color plates, many of them unpublished and re-coloured by our team of expert artists and scholars of uniformology. Each volume is based on 100 color plates or more, always accompanied by the original translated text which describes the subjets of the plates.

A unique work in its genre, a must have in any respecting collection!

Aleksandr Vasilevich Viskovatov born 22 April (4 May New Style) 1804, died 27 February (11 March) 1858 in St. Petersburg, Russian military historian. He graduated from the 1st Cadet Corps and served in the artillery, the hydrographic depot of the Naval Ministry, and then in the Department of Military Educational Institutions.

He mainly studied historical artifacts and the histories of military units. Viskovatov's greatest work was the Historical Description of the Clothing and Arms of the Russian Army (Vols. 1-30, St. Petersburg, 1841-62; 2nd ed. Vols. 1-34, St. Petersburg - Novosibirsk - Leningrad, 1899-1948). This work is based on a great quantity of archival documents and contains four thousand colored illustrations.

Viskovatov was the author of Chronicles of the Russian Army (Books 1-20, St. Petersburg, 1834-42) and Chronicles of the Russian Imperial Army (Parts 1-7, St. Petersburg, 1852). He collected valuable material on the history of the Russian navy which went into A Short Overview of Russian Naval Campaigns and General Voyages to the End of the XVII Century (St. Petersburg, 1864; 2nd edition Moscow, 1946). Together with A.I. Mikhailovskii-Danilevskii he helped prepare and create the Military Gallery in the Winter Palace.

He wrote the historical military inscriptions for the walls of the Hall of St. George in the Great Palace of the Kremlin. (From the article in the Soviet Military Encyclopedia.)

CONTENTS

*

THE WESTER UNIFORMS OF PETER THE GREAT'S ARMY

By Boris Megorsky (with is grateful permission)

The introduction of Western costume in Russia was a part of Peter the Great's reforms and, as such, it has been subject to research by many authors. However, research never ends and new evidence keeps surfacing that helps to adjust, refresh and update our view on a typical *"Petrine"* soldier. Based on first hand sources and the most recent academic research, as well as on illustrations and surviving relics of the period, the author proposes corrections to the contemporary common understanding on how elements of the costume - headgear, dress and footwear - looked like, and what were the authentic ways of wearing it.

Introduction

The first study of uniforms of Tsar Peter's army was published in 1842 by A.V. Viskovatov in the 2nd volume of a multi-volume *"The Historical description of dress and armament of Russian troops"*.

The uniforms in it were described based on few first-hand documents, illustrations and surviving artifact. Some details about regimental uniform colors were given in the Appendix to the volume. However, sources used by the author were scarce and the authentic pieces weren't described correctly. Thus the resulting research by Viskovatov came out rather superficial and illustrations drawn to supplement his work were unreliable. Still it was reprinted in 1899 and remained the only source of knowledge about Petrine uniforms for readers from 1840-s until 1990-s. Viskovatov was (and even still is) the most readily available and the most broadly known authority about the subject. And because of that, all third-hand literature including that published elsewhere in the world kept on reproducing and circulating the details that were not necessarily reliable.

Many first-hand sources about Petrine army including documents related to uniforms were published in late 19th – early 20th centuries in numerous collections of archival documents, regimental histories etc. However no one then attempted to consider these materials in order to correct Viskovatov's work. The breakthrough in the Russian uniformology happened only in the last two decades, when new scholars like S. Karpuschenko, S. Letin, V. Egorov, K. Tatarnikov, I. Ulyanov and O. Leonov started using new documents, memoires and archival sources. Links to their works are listed in the end of the article. So the research of Petrine uniforms goes on, albeit it is hindered by following obstacles:

- The surviving costumes as a rule belonged to high ranking persons. For example, the so called "Wardrobe of Peter the Great" is probably the largest known collection of male dress of early 18th century. It is stored in State Hermitage in St. Petersburg with some of its' pieces dispersed across other minor museums. But it belonged to a ruling monarch while there are nearly no surviving items of Russian soldiers' or officers' uniforms or equipment;

- The period documents about uniforms as a rule have little information required to re-create details; the cut, construction, dimensions or color are rarely mentioned;

- Considerable part of pre-1711 regimental documents were lost in the Turkish Prut River campaign, so we have far better sources on uniforms after 1711;

- The period illustrations are very few and show little detail; period prints, paintings or bas-reliefs of Russian soldiers exist but it is hard to tell whether they are original eyewitness drawings or they are just copied samples of European artists.

The Russian army entered Great Northern War 1700 – 1721 (GNW) in uniforms of Eastern type often referred to as Hungarian dress. It was some sort of a combination of Russian, Polish and Hungarian costume and it is subject to research and discussion of scholars, reenactors and artists today – we will leave it to them and only recommend recent articles and illustrations by Sergey Shamenkov dedicated to the subject and published on www.milhist.info. The text you are reading is dedicated to the Western uniforms introduced by Tsar Peter – it's elements, manner of wearing and so on as they are known from period sources. In a nutshell the purpose of the undertaken work is, giving due credit to other researchers, to reveal and discard deeply rooted misconceptions about Petrine uniforms that still exist today and keep being copied by generations of less informed artists, miniaturists and reenactors.

THE EUROPEAN DRESS IN RUSSIAN ARMY 1702 - 1721

The first set of Western style uniforms was manufactured for Russian troops on the occasion of the triumphant return to Moscow in December 1702 after the victorious campaign and siege of Noteborg in October. The manufacturing was done in haste, wool of chosen colors was purchased, 'German-style' stockings were hard to find on Russian market, buttons on this first occasion were covered with cloth and no more than total 500 kits were prepared for the parade for both guard regiments: The Preobrazhensky Guard Regiment received dark green coats with red facings, the Semenovsky Guard Regiment received blue with red facings; a third infantry regiment was seen on the same parade in red uniforms where half of the men wore Western style and the other half wore old style coats. This was the first time when the Russian army was dressed in Western garb in public and it was starting point from where troops started receiving new uniforms. The transition took some time and not all regiments received new kits at once. Several foreign witness accounts in 1704 recorded that all Russian units observed near Dorpat, Narva and in Poland wore German style. Still in January 1705, British envoy Charles Whitworth witnessed an infantry regiment in which officers wore Western coats and the soldiers wore some sort of Russian native dress. In general it is believed that by 1705 most of the Russian field army received Western style uniforms. The costume kit included a coat, a waistcoat worn underneath, short trousers, stockings, shoes, neckcloth and a hat.

Hat

The broad brimmed hats weren't popular in Russia until introduction of Western costume. They were manufactured out of a wool felt, and their quality and price depended on what raw material was used. The beaver (castor) hats had the finest quality and were most expensive, while soldiers' hats were made of more raw and cheap wool.

The hat crown as seen on most of contemporary illustrations and on surviving hats of Peter I and Charles XII had cylinder shape and a flat top. It was not sphere as modern artwork or replicas often tends to show. Inside hats had lining that in 1709 in one of hat factories they used black linen for it. The brim width was not regulated in the early years, at least no such prescriptions are known to us. The surviving items and iconography show both broad and narrow brims.

And the earliest known regulation dates back to 1730s and prescribed brims from 11 to 13.2 centimeters. Hat brims may have been trimmed with lace, but there is no specification of the lace used for trimming in early years. In December 1702, at the parade mentioned above, guards had hats trimmed with white lace; similar observation was made at a parade in 1703. In 1706 wool cloth was used to trim hats of the Preobrazhensky Regiment: 7 companies used wool 'from rotten coats', other companies received wool from Smolensk; and we don't know what was its color.

Hat lace was only regulated in 1720s when it was to be 2.2 centimeters broad white wool lace. According to a report of uniforms chancellery, in 1708-1709 twelve regiments received new hats but only 3 of them received white hat lace.

The cockade in early 18th century was a bow of colored ribbons. Cockades weren't typical in Russian uniforms during the Great Northern War, later in the century it was white cockade.

According to a Swedish intelligence report dated 1717, one infantry regiment – Ingermanlandsky – had pink (!) cockades on their hats. No information is known in documents about lace loops and buttons on Russian hats; one can often see in illustrations a button sewn on left brim of a hat. The fashion of wearing hats changed over time: brims were turned upwards from one side first and then from several sides and formed so called cocked hat or tricorn.

There is interesting letter in Peter's correspondence in 1706. The Tsar, being a Colonel of the Preobrazhensky Guard Regiment, was shown a model hat that was proposed for the regiment.

He wrote that the hat was good but it had four (!) corners while it should had had three corners as was fashionable then.

It should be noted that contemporary prints often do not show tricorns but instead show rather lose hats where brims weren't attached firmly to the crown. A document from hat factory tells that certain length of cord and knitted buttons was allocated for production of one hat; perhaps these were used to attach brims to crown. One could tighten the cord or loosen it so that brims fell down and cover the soldiers' shoulders from the rain. Hat felt was stiffened with glue which, however, was washed out by rain and hats lost their fancy shape. The cocked hat was worn, as a rule, corner forward. However in this case the left corner touched the musket carried on left shoulder, so the front corner was shifted slightly to the left eyebrow.

Kartuz

Another headgear typical for Russian army during GNW was kartuz – a soft cloth cap with peak and flaps. Compared to a felt hat it was a far more comfortable wear for colder climates and was popular in the Swedish army as "karpus" and was also known in 17th century Europe as Montero cap.

Several caps of this type survived in the Tsar's wardrobe in Hermitage.

As seen on surviving items, the kartuz had varying shapes of crown, flaps and peak (none of them, however, resembles caps shown in Viskovatov). A decoration on the cap included lace.

According to period documents, flaps had buttons but it is hard to tell where exactly they were. The earliest known mention of kartuzes in the Russian army was brought up in 1706 in correspondence between the Tsar and Alexander Menshikov. In 1708 in a letter that summarized what uniforms should look like in the army, Peter wrote that kartuz was the preferable headwear for soldiers.

After this letter, caps started being formally introduced to the troops. Danish envoy Just Jul witnessed a Russian infantry regiment (Colonel Fichtengeim) returning from Poltava in 1709 'in Swedish headwear'. Those might have been either trophy karpuses or Russian kartuzes that the Dane hadn't seen before on Muskovites. The kartuz became most widespread in the Russian army during 1710-s. In 1711 a new headgear was manufactured for 18 regiments: only 5 of them received hats and 13 received kartuzes. However later in 1720 the kartuz was abandoned in the army and replaced with the hat. In comparison with the hat, the kartuz provided better cover from cold, wind and snow.

But in summer it was excessively warm and did not adequately protect from the sun, and in bad weather it did not cover the shoulders from rain. Moreover, the kartuz was more expensive to manufacture than the hat.

In this period there were no regulations about having special headwear for fatigue. The kartuz was not analogous to fatigue caps of later periods, it was the only full dress headwear for many regiments that didn't have hats. In some regiments hats were few and were only issued to non-commissioned officers. One case is known where soldiers of the St. Petersburg garrison were issued hats before going on guard duty while they wore the kartuz in their daily routines.

Grenadier Cap

Men of the grenadier companies or regiments wore a specific headgear – tall and narrow caps that, unlike broad brimmed hats, allowed the soldier to sling a musket over his shoulder (which was necessary manipulation before igniting and throwing a grenade).

There were no regulation model grenadier caps throughout the years of the Great Northern War, so every regimental commander (or General of a Division) could have ordered manufacture of headgear of his own preference for his men; so the end result most likely depended on Colonel's taste, contemporary fashion, available resources and orders of higher command.

The first depiction of a Russian grenadier cap was printed in 1698 in so called 'Manual of Adam Weide'. The cap in that Manual was a fur cylinder with no decorations.

It isn't known yet who were soldiers depicted in this Manual so this well might be a fictional image but we also may assume this sort of cap might have been in use in the late 17th century.

In European armies fur caps with soft cloth bags were popular in early 1700s and this fashion was adopted in Russia too. Sources tell that in 1703 bombardiers of Preobrazhensky Guard Regiment wore "german caps with big black fur trimming"; in 1707 grenadiers of same regiment had caps with red cloth tops and bearskin capbands; and in 1711 Preobrazhensky again received bearskin caps. There are a couple of contemporary Russian pictures that show some sort of caps with low fur capbands, although it is not known for sure whether these particular models were worn by grenadiers.

Grenadier caps made of leather were first mentioned in documents of the Guards in 1706, however they weren't introduced then. It is only in 1712 that we know leather grenadier helmets complete with front flap with tin plate, rear peak and ostrich feathers were introduced for grenadier companies of both Guard regiments. The construction of the cap was supposed to resemble an ancient Roman helmet. A number of such grenadier helmets has survived from first half of 18th century and they also

The Emperor Peter the Great at work with his soldiers (Khudoyarov, Vassily Pavlovich) (1831-1892)

can be seen in period pictures. In 1719, 412 ostrich feathers were purchased for the two grenadier companies: 12 were white and were most likely for officers, others were red. The helmets were purchased in England although we don't know if similar caps were in use anywhere else in Europe.

A unique surviving grenadier cap of Petrine times is stored today in a collection of the Suvorov Museum in St. Petersburg. It has front and rear flaps and tall top curved backwards.

The flaps are decorated with embroidery of a double eagle, grenades, ciphers and crossed swords and bayonets. According to a hypothesis of Sergey Letin, this cap might have belonged to the 2nd Grenadier Regiment (Col. Du Boy). Period documents mention caps of a similar decoration of red, blue and green textile made either for foot or dragoon grenadier regiments around 1709.

Similar caps seem to have been widespread in European armies in early 1700s.

Another type of grenadier cap for line regiments was a mitre cap with tall conical top and low flaps. The pointed top looked upwards and perhaps could be bent forward or backwards.

This type of cap became popular during 1710-20, and there are surviving items from the 1730s.

The mitre caps are shown on another bas-relief by Rastrelli and Nartov on a medallion dedicated for the battle of Dobroe in 1708. The composition and figures on the medallion were taken from Louis Laguerre's painting showing the battle of Blenheim, 1704 with grenadiers and musketeers crossing a river. The Russian artist Nartov, who travelled to England during 1718-19, was probably acquainted with Laguerre's work and copied it. However he gave new caps to grenadiers – several figures wear leather helmets of a guards pattern and some wear mitres with decorations different from those on British grenadiers (out of four seams on the top one seam is located in center front).

This means that likely this type of cap was typical to Russian grenadiers in the years when the bas-relief was created. The tall red caps with low white flaps were made model grenadier caps in the 1720s and perhaps existed some time prior to that. In order to preserve the richly decorated caps they used waxed textile covers.

◄ Grenadiers in leather guard helmets and in tall mitre caps.

Fragment of a bas-relief depicting the battle of Dobroe, 1708. by Rastrelli, Bartholomeo Carlo (1675 – 1744); Nartov, Andrey Konstantinovich (1693 – 1756)) Hermitage Museum.

Photograph by Boris Megorsky.

A big set of brass round medallions and long plates, all in bas-relief technique, was created in the 1720s by Rastrelli and his team. They showed all the key actions of the Great Northern War and were to constitute decoration of a Triumphant column which remained a project.

Besides embroidery and decorative applications, grenadier caps also had metal front plates. For example, in the Butyrsky Regiment in December 1696, General Patrick Gordon ordered plates of white tin. Tin plates were for lower ranks of Guard grenadiers while officers had silver plates on their caps. There is little information about what were details of those plates' decoration. Period European drawings show plates in a shape of a grenade on their fur caps and the metal plates of the guard grenadiers bore a double eagle. Such was the variety of grenadier caps that were in use in the years of the Great Northern War and it is hard to tell for sure what type and what color was worn in what regiment and in what years. An assumption would be that in the early 1700s, the most popular were textile caps with a curved top or bearskins and later in the 1710s, line grenadiers received mitre caps and guard grenadiers received leather helmets.

Hairstyle

The Military Regulation of Peter the Great read that the company feldsher (doctor's assistant) was to shave soldiers once a week. There are tsar's letters where he ordered soldiers to shave before parades. Wearing moustaches was not prescribed then, but according to period illustrations it was fashionable to have them upwards. Drawings show soldiers wearing long hair that covered ears and touched their shoulders. Period illustrations show soldiers of various European armies that wore lose hair, or had hair gathered behind and fixed with a ribbon or put in a bag. Another style was to tuck the hair ends upwards under the hat. These fashions are mentioned in documents of the Russian army in the 1720s but there were no regulations about hairstyle prior to that. We can only safely presume that soldiers did not cover their hair with white powder, did not wear queues and did not wear wigs. Officers did wear wigs, though.

Neck cloth

This accessory was a necessary part of period costume. Contemporary illustrations depict rather narrow pieces of cloth.; When the neck cloth was first regulated in Russian documents around the mid-18th century, it was to be one "vershok" (44 millimeters) broad and it looks like the same applied to earlier periods. Some period images show neck ties or scarves with lose ends hanging in front. There is one document that mentions length of neck cloth manufactured for artillery (gunners attached to dragoon regiments) in 1708 at 140 centimeters long. This ribbon was wrapped around neck, tied in front or on the back and its lose ends either showed over the coat or were tucked to under coat or waistcoat.

In 1708, the Tsar ordered that soldiers were to be issued with a short black neck cloth with a fastening. It meant that the neck cloths were to be only as long as needed to encircle the neck once and its ends were connected on the back with hooks or a buckle or with plain cords. The most popular textile for neck cloth was "trip" – a fleecy wool fabric.

Uniform Colors

As units of the army wore all varieties of colors in the course of war, it was hard to tell what colors were worn by certain regiments in a particular year. Until recently one could only find this information in the Appendix to Viskovatov. The data was rather fragmentary and most often it only covered the period after 1711. In that year the Russian army lost its equipment trains, including regimental chancelleries, in the unlucky campaign on the Pruth River..

The most comprehensive information about Russian uniforms, weapons and equipment available nowadays, albeit not exhaustive due to limitations of sources, was published in 2008 in a book by archivists from Moscow, written by Kirill Tatarnikov and edited by Vadim Egorov.

They worked through surviving regimental chancelleries stored in Russian State Military-Historical Archive (RGVIA).

Another valuable source about regimental uniform colors was published by Swedish authors Lars-Eric Höglund and Åke Sallnäs in the 2nd volume of their reference book 'The Great Northern War 1700-1721. Colours and Uniforms'. It is based in part on reports of Swedish agents and spies who observed Russian troops in Ingermanland and Finland. Their data is sketchy but still very useful.

Rarely some more information about uniform colors of particular regiments can be found in memoirs, official reports or correspondence.

The concept of national colors of military uniforms only started to appear in our period.

In 1708 Tsar Peter wrote that green was the preferred color for soldiers' coats, however the diversity of uniform colors was considerable in Russian army of the Great Northern War period.

They varied from such traditional shades like green, blue, white and red to more unusual like yellow (was proposed for Menshikov's Ingermanland Infantry Regiment in 1706 but it wasn't carried out) or 'dead flowers' (brownish-yellow, as observed by Danish envoy in Russian garrison at Narva in 1709).

The same regiment might change colors every two or three years, when new uniforms were issued and manufactured out of wool of whatever color was available at that moment. Few units retained same colors throughout whole war years. The few known that did are the Preobrazhensky Guard Regiment – green, the Semenovsky Guard Regiment – blue, the elite infantry regiments Butyrsky and Lefortovsky– red.

While regiments may have differed one from another in color, they aimed to keep uniformity within one unit. On several occasions NCOs had coats of different colors than other ranks.

Most of the colored wool cloth was imported from England, Hamburg or Lubeck and when this became in short supply, they started to dye white or grey wool cloth manufactured in Russia.

First, they dyed in a green color and in 1706 in Menshikov's correspondence there's mention of dying using birch leaves. Sometimes undyed cloth was issued, however most likely this was reserved for non-combatants, officers' servants and train drivers – there are several known instructions about that from 1705 - 1711.

Despite occasional color diversity, green remained predominant color for Russian infantry and eventually became distinctive color of Russian uniforms, rarely found in other armies.

Coat

The main part of costume that received the French name "just au corps" was developed in Europe in the late third of the 17th century and it became universal to many stratas of society, including the military. The western coat differed from eastern coats with its cut, details (large cuffs, massive folds and pleats in the skirt, pocket flaps) and length (the skirt touched ground if man stood on knees). When referring to Western costume, Russian documents of the period mention 'German', 'French' and 'Saxon' dress; however today it is hard to tell for sure what differences contemporaries saw between them. Period illustrations and survived items present relatively similar cut of coats all over

Portrait of Peter I attributed to Jean Marc Nattier 1685-1766 (Hermitage S.Peterburg)

Europe. Some details like cuffs, pockets, collars or fastening, their shape and position might change but the overall silhouette of a coat remained the same.

The skirt of a coat was cut as a broad 'fan' and then gathered in folds on both sides. This created the peculiar feature of the period costume - a knee long bell shape skirt beneath the waist.

In order to ease horse riding they used to turn corners of the skirt and fasten them together with hooks and holes – thus turnbacks of facing color were seen. Such a practice can be found on period images in the 1700s, however in Russian army it probably became widespread only in the 1720s.

Particulars of coat cut are rarely found in available period documents, however some mention that in early years the coats in the Russian army were double breasted (had 'double buttons', i.e. both sides of the breast had buttons and loopholes). Breasts had color lining all the way down and could form lapels if fastened with buttons. As seen in some iconography, lapels could be fixed with topmost buttons only, thus forming small triangular lapels. Another method was to turn the lapels along all of the breast until the bottom of the skirt. Alternatively, a breast could be all fastened so that no color lapels were seen. According to the Tsar's correspondence, the Preobrazhensky Guard Regiment was the first to get single breasted coats in 1708, but some regiments were known to a wear double breasted pattern as late as 1711.

A unique portrait of 'the first Russian soldier' Bukhvostov shows a coat of a slightly different pattern that has a double breast only until the waist, thus forming large triangular lapels. Similar lapels are found on some European period drawings of the 1700–1720s.

The majority of the period visual sources, however, show single breasted coats. This type constitutes also the vast majority of surviving items in museum collections. It looks like in Russian army it came in use after 1708. The tendency seen on illustrations says that in early 18th century, it was more common to have button holes all along the breast. In 1708, when Peter gave instructions on the manufacture of new coats to the Preobrazhensky Guard Regiment, he prescribed it as single breasted and to cut holes only until the waist. Peter's own coat worn by him at the Poltava battle in 1709 was cut this way. Button holes might have been trimmed with color cloth or cord.

Numerous buttons and cut through button holes were typical feature of a European coat. Besides fastening on the breast, there were buttons on other parts of the coat like cuffs, pockets, in folds and on waist. Overall quantity and position of those buttons changed over time. There are no known exhaustive regulations on this matter, however there are a number of references in various documents that help: 36 buttons on a dragoon coat in 1706, 26 buttons in 1709 for the Semenovsky Guard Regiment; 18 buttons in 1717 for line infantry.

Uniforms buttons were most often hollow brass (two parts soldered together) or cast tin or covered with cloth. Buttons as a rule had plain surface but those bearing double eagle were also issued.

The quantity of buttons on the breast of the coats of the Preobrazhensky Guard Regiment depended on coat size (12 buttons on large coats, 11 buttons on medium). In line regiments, however, amount of buttons was fixed irrespective to the size.

Most often buttons and holes were evenly distributed along the breast, but sometimes one can see on European period drawings that buttons were grouped together (two of three buttons in a group) with a gap between groups; this manner didn't become popular in Russian military costume.

In early years, the coats had a low standing upright collar of the same color as the coat – as seen on Peter's coat worn at Poltava or there was no collar at all. Turndown collars are found in some documents as early as 1706, probably it became widespread in uniforms during the 1710s. Sleeves, according to fashion of the period, were rather baggy in 1700s and became tighter later on.

Sleeve cuffs on period pictures and surviving items tended to be round (without slit) in early 1700s and with slits later in the 1710s; so called 'brandenburg' cuffs with a flap was another type of cuffs of the period, albeit not so often seen on Russian uniforms. A presumption of Sergey Letin is that only guards had buttons on their cuffs – and this explained why the overall amount of buttons on coats for guard and line regiments differed.

Pockets were located on fore part of a skirt and were covered with flaps of varying shape. Horizontal pockets - were more common – had flaps which varied from narrow and nearly rectangular in early years to pentagonal or with some curved edge. According to visual sources, pockets were positioned rather low in early 1700s and later on they lifted up towards waist line, where breast fastening ended. In European, including Swedish, uniforms one could find vertical pockets, however there was hardly this type in Russian uniforms. Shoulder straps were merely functional and were not insignia in those years. Those were pieces of cloth or cord often on the left shoulder only to fix the shoulder belts of equipment. A few descriptions of shoulder straps are found in documents during the 1720s only.

Waistcoat

This garment named "kamzol" in period texts was worn under the coat and as such it was barely seen at all. Later in 18th century the waistcoat became shorter, losing its sleeves and eventually became a vest. But in early 1700s it resembled a coat in cut, it was only palm-wide shorter, had a smaller skirt and had no cuffs on the sleeves.

Fashion of the period allowed that the waistcoat was seen from under the coat and shirt and the neck cloth were seen from under waistcoat. So, when the weather allowed, it was not unusual to have a coat unfastened or fastened only by a few lower buttons. The waistcoat, too, might have been fastened on less than all buttons. Waistcoats had smaller buttons than the coats and surviving documents mention these buttons separately from larger coat buttons. Their quantity varied over time as well: there are mentions of 22 buttons on waistcoat in 1704, 26 in 1706, 18 in 1717 and 21 in 1720.

From the visual sources, they wore a waistbelt (or port-epee) over the waistcoat (and thus under the coat) or over the coat. Later in the mid18th century there were regulations in the Russian army that prescribed having a waistbelt over a waistcoat in the summertime and over a coat in the wintertime; no such regulations in the early 1700s are known. In the summertime it was possible to wear only a waistcoat without a coat at all and there are a few references of this in period document and illustration, however it is hard to tell if that was common practice during the Great Northern War. Early in the 1700s, the waistcoats were issued to the troops along with the rest of the uniforms. When short supply of quality wool became obvious, they started to save costs. In 1707, Peter ordered that waistcoats were to be manufactured out of grey or white undyed Russian wool or out of old coats. One year later, this practice was put into regulation. Waistcoats were then to be made within regiments out of old coats or cloaks. The guards, however, kept their red waistcoats.

Trousers

Trousers were little longer than knee height, were rather spacious in the seat and hence a lot of folds in the rear. Two types of fastening were used then: with front flap (bearer) and with a fly. Majority of the surviving Tsar's trousers have slits and buttons on lower end of trouser legs, however lower ranks had mere draw string on trouser legs, with neither cuffs nor buttons. Like the waistcoats, trousers were initially made of quality color wool but later they shifted to less expensive textile. In 1708-1709 trousers were made out of "aba" a Russian made white wool. But as long as trousers were to be durable, they returned to tougher material. In 1710, trousers were made of quality color wool or out of leather. Woolen trousers were too thick and were especially uncomfortable during the summer heat. Leather was durable and practical but it's quality depended on the manufacturer. Elk or deer skins manufactured by craftsmen in Narva or Reval were of better quality and more expensive. Goatskin manufactured by Russian craftsmen was cheaper but was more susceptible to effects of heat and wet. In any case, leather trousers were widespread in Russian infantry during the 1710s.

Stockings

Stockings probably existed in Russian pre-Petrine costume, although they differed from their Western version When in autumn of 1702 the Tsar ordered the manufacture of 500 Western uniform kits, it turned out that it was hard to find as many 'German style' stockings red in color. In order to complete the task in time they gathered stockings of whatever shades close to red that were available. There is a steady myth about introducing red stockings to the guards after their distinction in the unfortunate Narva 1700 battle, but it is not supported by sources. The most common colors of stockings that were issued in the Russian army during the Great Northern War were red, blue or more cheap white or grey.

Two pairs of stocking in a year were due to a soldier per the 1708 regulation. Those were most often knitted of woolen thread, but were also cut and sewn, and even felted stockings were not unheard of. In an emergency they could make stockings out of old canvas tents, as Peter ordered to the Preobrazhensky Guard Regiment in 1712.

According to the period illustrations, stocking were long enough to cover knee and were worn over trousers. A garter – leather or textile belt with a buckle – was wrapped around the leg under the knee and kept the stockings in place.

Gaiters

Prince Boris Kurakin, officer of the Semenovsky Guard Regiment and later a leading Russian diplomat, travelled in Europe and in 1706 recorded that he saw Prussian grenadiers who had some sort of canvas covers over their stockings. This observation probably means that this item was not known in Russian uniforms by then. Originally, this was merely a utilitarian item and did not belong to the full dress. It preserved feet from mud, cold and water and preserved the stockings from wearing out on campaign. The first mention of covers is found in December 1707 when Fieldmarshall Boris Sheremetiev ordered that his troops prepare for the winter campaign and make a "Stiefelette" out of skins of slaughtered bulls. In 1712, the Tsar recommended that gaiters should be made out of old canvas tents. It is believed that gaiters became widespread in the Russian army after the1712 campaign in North Germany.

Gaiters were manufactured within regiments out of local supplies so at first there were no regulations as to their dimensions or appearance. From period depictions from both Europe and Russia, gaiters just like stockings, were above the knee long and were fixed with a garter. Unlike the stocking, the gaiter had a side fastening on the outer seam (12 buttons) and a flap that covered the shoe, thus preventing mud, rocks or snow from filling in the shoes).

Shoes

This most typical footwear was an ankle high black shoe which had a thick sole and a high heel. Two pairs of shoes were issued (or were to be issued) to a soldier in a year. Toe shape varied – pointed or round toe cap can be found among text documents, period illustrations and surviving items, however a rectangular shape seems to have been most popular. It is known that in 1720s such shoes were issued to foot soldiers while shoes with pointed toes were issued to sailors. A shoe had a long tongue and two side latchets. The later were fastened with a buckle or with a lacing. A Tsar's letter from 1708 mentions sending shoes without buckles and with laces to the army. In December 1711, Peter explicitly wrote that supply of shoe buckles should be stopped because in

▲ Equestrian portrait of Empress Catherine I (1684-1727) by Georg Cristoph Grooth 1716-1749 (Kadrioru kunstimuuseum)

other armies the soldiers had tie-laces instead of buckles on their shoes. Nevertheless, documents show that shoe buckles were still sent to regiments during 1710-20 in considerable numbers.

Although left and right shoes were known then, for economy the army cut soles without distinction between the two. Soldiers thus wore identical shoes on both feet. Some particulars of such footwear can be found in a document by Alexander Suvorov when he was an infantry Colonel in the 1760s. It was recommended that soldiers interchange the shoe from right foot to left and back again which helped soles and heels wear out evenly and last longer. In wintertime, straw was put inside the shoes to prevent cold. Shortages of footwear were not uncommon during the war. It is known that soldiers wore out their shoes during the 1708 campaign and by autumn had to make footwear on their own out of some old skins. In 1712 General Adam Weide reported that soldiers of his division had their only pair of shoes worn out in 9 months and many were barefoot.

High boots

The most popular concept of an 18th century soldier shows figure in shoes and stockings or gaiters. However, in Russian army high boots were also issued to infantry, one pair in a year. Little is known about outlook of this item in Great Northern War. A few documents mention that boots were made of cowhide leather and had a round or pointed toe cap. A document from 1706 says "German style boots," whatever it meant, were supplied to troops. East European boots – both civilian and military – with a pointed toe cap and soft bootleg can be found in both visual sources and archeology. The "German" i.e. West European boots can be found today in many collections as cavalry boots from the 17th – 18th centuries, with square toes, sturdy high bootlegs, knee flaps and high heels. Infantry kept on wearing high boots from the 1700s until later in the 1760s when the same aforementioned document by Suvorov described them a little. The boots had high, over knee long, bootlegs of soft leather. The top could be pulled down to below knee but the bootleg was held upright with pullstraps that were attached to the garter. One can speculate that same boot construction was in use in the course of first half of the century.

The two guard regiments together with few elite line infantry regiments became mounted infantry for a certain period of time during the war, from 1707 to 1712. They had to be fast enough in order to follow the Tsar who was rushing from one theater of war to another. They only marched mounted but after they arrived to battlefield they dismounted and fought as infantry. In any case, these regiments were issued dragoon equipment, including dragoon high boots. There is a number of documents with lists of uniforms and equipment of guard regiments during those years and often mention supply or loss of high boots, none mention shoes. It could be that guards perhaps had privately purchased shoes that weren't in the regimental records. Another possibility is that they had only boots then and later at Poltava they fought in high boots, contrary to the conventional view of guardsmen in red stockings.

Cloak

A cape with broad turndown collar was to cover the men from cold and rain. Cloaks were made of wool and lined with color canvas at shoulders, breasts and rear slit. The only fastening was a hook and loop buckle at the neck. This garb wasn't too comfortable. The collar was not broad enough to cover the head from wind or rainfall and the breast was open and there were no sleeves.

They maintained the same color of cloaks for guard units throughout the years of the Great Northern War. The Preobrazhensky Guard Regiment had dark green, and the Semenovsky Guard Regiment had blue with a red lining. Line regiments' cloak color changed over time and it depended on whatever wool was available when it came time to manufacture new uniforms. The Tsar recommended in 1708 to make cloaks out of "plain," i.e. grey or white wool, once every 3 years. In fact, in that very year four regiments received green and red cloaks and six regiments received grey cloaks with red, blue or yellow lining. During 1710-20, it was common to have cloaks of green, red and blue wool with red, blue, green, white or yellow lining. The collar of the cloak was in the facing color in the 1720s, however that is unlikely to have been the case from 1700 to 1710. When a soldier did not wear his cloak or left it on the equipment train, he carried it with him in a roll. Prince Kurakin in his memoirs left a mention of this way of carrying the cloak in the Prussian army in 1706. Still, the first known evidence of Russian soldiers to carry cloak in a roll over the shoulder is a drawing of artillerist from 1720s.

Just like what happened with other items of uniforms, there were often interruptions in issuing new cloaks to the troops. For example, an order to manufacture 18,000 cloaks for 15 infantry regiments was given in May 1708, however only 10,000 cloaks were ready by February 1709.; This means that the soldiers spent most of winter time without cloaks. In 1712, General Adam Weide was complaining to Tsar that men of his Division didn't have cloaks and in consequence their coats wore out sooner than was expected. The appearance of troops was often far from ideal. The timely arrival of new uniforms was hindered by shortage of textiles or by slowness of the bureaucratic systems responsible for supplies. So it was not uncommon for soldiers to wear old, worn out, faded and torn uniforms. Even the Semenovsky Regiment (the Guards!) was to receive new uniforms in the summer of 1708, but the cloaks arrived only in January and coats with waistcoats were expected to arrive in February 1709.

▲ Portrait of Empress Anna Ioannovna (1730) by Louis Caravaque,

FURTHER READING

Tatarnikov, Kirill. (2008) *The Russian Field Army 1700 – 1730. Uniforms and Equipment [Russkaya polevaya armiya 1700 – 1730. Obmundirovanie i snaryazhenie].* [The most exhaustive complex work on supplies of the Petrine army, which includes uniforms and weapons data for nearly all foot and dragoon regiments. No illustrations, text in Russian, see link for free pdf]

Egorov, Vadim. (2011) *Uniforms of Petrine army 1706 – 1710 as per letters of A. D. Menshikov [Mundir petrovskoy armii 1706 -1710 v pis'makh A.D. Menshikova].* [article refines research of manuscripts, done before by Sergey Letin, dismisses the long living myth about yellow coats of Ingermanlandsky Infantry Regiment. It has a few illustrations, text in Russian,.

Letin, Sergey. 'The Service Dress of Peter the Great [Sluzhiloe platye ot Petra Velikogo]', *Rodina*, 2000, # 11. [Article on uniforms of the guard regiments. Author's illustrations, text in Russian, see link for free pdf]

Letin, Sergey. 'The war of camisols and padded jackets [Voina kamzolov i telogreyek]', *Imperiya Istorii*, 2002, # 3. [An illustrated review article on European military costume in the Petrine army. Text in Russian, see link for free text and images]

Letin, Sergey. (1995) *The Russian Military Costume in 18th Century. [Russkiy voenny kostyum XVIII veka]* [An overview book covering whole century, illustrated with some items' photos and portraits. Text in Russian, see link for free pdf]

Letin, Sergey, Leonov, Oleg. (2008) *The Russian Military Costume. From Peter I to Peter III. [Russkiy voenny kostyum. Ot Petra I do Petra III]* [An illustrated volume packed with Letin's illustrious drawings and photos of original items. Out of print, see link to publisher]

Ulyanov, Ilya, Leonov, Oleg. (1995) '*The Regular Infantry. Vol. 1. 1698 – 1801. [Regulyarnaya Pekhota. T. 1. 1698 – 1801]*' [An overview volume covering organization, tactics, uniforms, flags and weapons of Russian infantry. A huge step forward after Viskovatov. A lot of illustrations.]

Karpuschenko, Sergey 'On uniforms supplies of Russian artillerists in the Northern war 1700 – 1721 [O mundirnom dovolstvii russkikh artilleristov v Severnoi voine 1700 – 1721 gg.]', *Sbornik VIMAIV*, 1990, # 5. [The first modern uniformological study that went beyond Viskovatov, based on archives of Artillery Museum.]

Shamenkova, Olga. (2007) *The Military and Civilian Costume of Early 18th Century in Details. [Voennyi i grazhdanskyi kostyum nachala XVIII veka v detalyakh]* [A unique detailed photographs and charts of costume items belonging to Peter the Great, transferred from Hermitage to Poltava Museum. Text in Russian.]

Minchenkov, Sergey. (2007) *Sewing charts and practical recommendations on creating a Petrine uniforms for reenactors.* [Six graphic plates with description in Russian.]

Höglund, Lars-Eric, Sallnäs, Åke and Bespalov, Alexander. (2006) *The Great Northern War 1700 - 1721, II. Swedens Allies and Enemies. Colours and Uniforms.* [In terms of regimental uniform colors this became a breakthrough publication in the era after Viskovatov and before Tatarnikov. Of particular interest is Russian uniform data from Swedish spy reports from various years of the war. Illustrations. Text in English. Available for sale from the publisher]

Viskovatov, Alexander. (1899) '*The Historical description of dress and armament of Russian troops. Vol. 2. 1700 – 1725. [Istoricheskoe opisanie odezhdy i vooruzhenia rossiiskikh voisk. T. 2.]*' [The classics, illustrations and texts in it have been around for 150 years and are outdated now as compared to the latest researches listed above.]

Portrait of Peter I (Russian National Museum S.Petorbury)

РИСУНКИ

одежды и вооруженiя

РОССIЙСКИХЪ

ВОЙСКЪ.

PLATES LIST OF ILLUSTRATIONS

Clothing and weapons of the Russian troops, with the addition of information on banners, signs of distinction in the reign of: Emperor Peter the Great from 1700 to 1725. Empress Catherine Ith from 1725 to 1727 year. Emperor Peter II from 1727 to 1730. The Empress Anna Ioannovna from 1730 to 1740

vonia, conquered by the Russian troops in 1702.

183 - Grenadier Infantry Regiment, in 1700 to 1732.

184 - Grenadier Shapka Army and Garrison regiments, from 1700 to 1732.

185 - Swords of the Army and Garrison Officers, from 1700 to 1732.

186 - Officer of the Infantry Regiment, from 1700 to 1732. The view depicts the time part of the St. Petersburg side, with the Cathedral of the Holy Trinity, the living-room, the fairy-tale colleges and the house that served the residence of Peter the Great, at the base of the SP-burg.

187 - Fusilier Dragoon Regiment, from 1700 to 1720.

188 - Dragoons' Palashas, from 1700 to 1732.

189 - Dragoons' sword from 1700 to 1732.

190 - Dragoons' sling with a hook and a saddle with an elm, from 1700 to 1732.

191 - Officer of the Dragoon Regiment, from 1700 to 1732. The view depicts the time the fortress of Yamburg. .

192 - The Dragoon Timpani, from 1700 to 1732. from 1712 to 1732.

193 – officer, bombardier and fusilier of the Artillery Regiment, from 1712 to 1720. The view depicts part of the Kremlin wall and Arsenal, in Moscow.

194 - Halberd and hand mortar bombardier of the Artillery Regiment, from 1712 to 1732.

195 - Sergeant and Fusilier L.-G. Preobrazhensky regiment, from 1720 to 1732.

196 - Fusilier L.-G. Semenovsky regiment, from 1720 to 1732.

197 - Officer L.-G. Semenovsky regiment, from 1720 to 1732.

198 - Fusilier Infantry of the Army Regiment, from 1720 to 1732.

199 - Fusilier of the Army Dragoon Regiment, from 1720 to 1732. The view depicts the time part of St. St. Petersburg Admiralty, the Church of St. Isaac of Dalmatia and the house of Prince Menshikov.

200 – Infantry Garrison Regiments, from 1720 to 1732. In the service and working clothes.

201 - Fusilier Dragoon Garrison Regiment, from 1720 to 1732.

202 - NCO of the Artillery Regiment, from 1720 to 1728.

203 – Ukrainian land milice, from 1713 to 1736 year.

204 – Cavalry Guards in 1724.

205 – Cavalry garde Timpani, 1724 and from 1726 to 1731.

206 - Little Russian Cossacks in the beginning of the XVIII century, Kazak registered or elected.

207 - Little Russian Cossacks in the beginning of the XVIII century, Cossack.

208 - Little Russian Cossacks in the beginning of the XVIII century, Cossack NCO.

209 - Little Russian Cossacks in the beginning of the XVIII century, Colonel.

210 – Zaporozhets in the XVIII century.

211 - The banner of L.-G. Preobrazhensky regiment, 1700 year.

212 - The banner of L.-G. Preobrazhensky regiment, 1700 year.

213 - The banner of L.-G. Preobrazhensky regiment, 1701 year.

214 - The banner of L.-G. Preobrazhensky regiment, 1701 year.

215 - The banner of L.-G. Semenovsky regiment, in 1701.

216 - The banner of L.-G. Preobrazhensky regiment, 1706 year.

217 - The banner of L.-G. Semenovsky regiment, 1701 year.

218 - The banner of L.-G. Semenovsky regiment, 1706 year.

219 - The banner of L.-G. Semenovsky regiment, 1706 year.

220 - The banner of L.-G. Preobrazhensky regiment, 1707 year.

221 - Banner of the regiments of L.-G. Preobrazhensky and Semenovsky on the 25th of February, 1711.

222 – 230 Banner of the Army Regiments, 1700-1727.

231 – Soldat and officer of the Leib-Regiment, from 1727 to 1730.

232 - The banner of L.-G. Preobrazhensky regiment, 1725-1727.

233 - The flag of the Leib-Regiment of 1726.

234 - Banner of the Army Regiment, 1727.

235 -Banner of the Army Regiment, February 16, 1727.

236 - Fusilier of the Artillery Regiment, from 1728 to 1732.

237 – Corporal, sergeant and officer of the Artillery Regiment, from 1728 to 1732.

238 - Musician of the Artillery Regiment, from 1728 to 1732.

239 – Officer and Ingenner of the Artillery Regiment, from 1728 to 1732. The view depicts the time a foundry barn, on the banks of the Neva River, in St. Petersburg, in place of the present foundry tower.

240 – Worker soldier of the Artillery Regiment, from 1728 to 1732.

241 - Profos Artillery Regiment, from 1728 to 1732 year.

242 – Conductor, men and worker of the Artillery Regiment, from 1728 to 1732.

243 - NCO Sign of L.-G. Preobrazhensky and Semenovsky regiments, 1727-1732.

244 - The banner of L.-G. Preobrazhensky regiment, 1727-1730.

245 - The banner of L.-G. Preobrazhensky regiment, 1727-1730.

246 – 247 - Banner of the 1st Moscow Regiment, 1727. The White Flag of the Army Regiment, which did not have its own coat of arms, November 11, 1727.

248 -249 The Banner of the Army Regiment, which had its own coat of arms, November 11, 1727. The Colored Flag of the Army Regiment, which did not have its coat of arms, November 11, 1727.

250 – 259 - The arms of the Army and Garrison regiments, approved on March 8, 1730.

260 – Musketeer of infantry 1732-1742

261 – Tricorne of Musketeer of infantry 1732-1742

262 – Sword and scabbard of officer from 1732 to 1742.

263 - Officer of the Infantry Regiment, from 1732 to 1742. The view depicts Sukharev Tower in Moscow.

264 – Sash, Partisan and gorged of officer from 1732 to 1742.

265 – Grenadier and NCO of an army uinfantry regiment from 1732 to 1742.

266 - Grenadier Shapka army and Garrison regiments from 1732 to 1756 year.

267 – Private of Dragoon Regiment, from 1732 to 1742.

268 - Officer of the Dragoon Regiment, from 1732 to 1742. The view depicts the time the Church of St. Isaac and the main Admiralty in the St.Petersburg.

269 - Grenadier of the Dragoon Regiment, from 1732 to 1742.

270 - Garrison regiments, from 1732 to 1742. In working and combat clothing. The view depicts the ruins of the castle of Ronneburg in Livonia.

271 – Private and Officer of the Cuirassier Regiments, from 1732 to 1742

272 - Officer and private of the Cuirassier Regiment, from 1732 to 1742.

273 - Cuirass of the lower ranks of the Cyrsir regiment, from 1732 to 1742.

274 - Cuirass of the Officers of the Cuirassier Regiments, from 1732 to 1742.

275 – Private and officer L.-G. Preobrazhensky Regiment, from 1732 to 1742.

276 - Grenadier OFFICER and Grenadier L.-G. Preobrazhensky Regiment, from 1732 to 1742.

277 – Men of the L.-G. The Semenovsky and the SL. L.-G. Izmaylovsky regiments, from 1732 to 1742.

278 – Officer of the L.-G. The Horse Regiment, from 1731 to 1742.

279 – Cuirass of the L.-G. The Horse Regiment, from 1732 to 1742.

280 – Land militia, from 1736 to 1742 year.

281 – Officers of land militia, from 1736 to 1742.

282 - Cadets Grenadier and Fusilier, from 1732 to 1742.

283 - Grenadier Shapka Cadet Corps, from 1735 to 1762 year.

284 - Cadet in the Horse Carriage, from 1732 to 1742. The view depicts a house, formerly the former Prince Menshikov, when he was appointed to the Cadet Corps in 1732.

285 - Cadet Supervest, from 1732 to 1762.

286 - Fusilier Officer of the Cadet Corps, from 1732 to 1742.

287 - Banner of the Army and Garrison Infantry Regiment, October 28, 1731. (The Butyrsky Regiment).

288 - Standard of the Cuirassier Regiment, 1731.

289 - The banner of L.-G. Preobrazhensky regiment, 1732-1742.

290 - The banner of L.-G. Izmaylovsky regiment, 1731 year.

291 - Monogrammed images of the name of Empress Anna Ioannovna, installed for the banners.

292 - The flag of the Fuselier mouth of the Cadet Corps, 1732-1760.

2923 - Standard of the Horse Company of the Cadet Corps, 1732.

The zar Peter the Great 1682-1725

Catherine I of Russia 1725-1727

Peter II 1727-1730

Anna Joannovna 1730-1740

Private in the years from 1700-to 1720.

Fusilier Preobrazhensky regiment, from 1700 to 1720. The view depicts part of the city and fortress of Narva, conquered by the Russian troops in 1704.

Fusilier L.-G. Preobrazhensky regiment, from 1700 to 1720. The view depicts a mazarkovaya structure on the banks of the Neva River, on the site of the current Dvortsovaya embankment in St. Petersburg, as it was in the first years of this city.

Headgears of Officers and Lower ranks, from 1700 to 1732

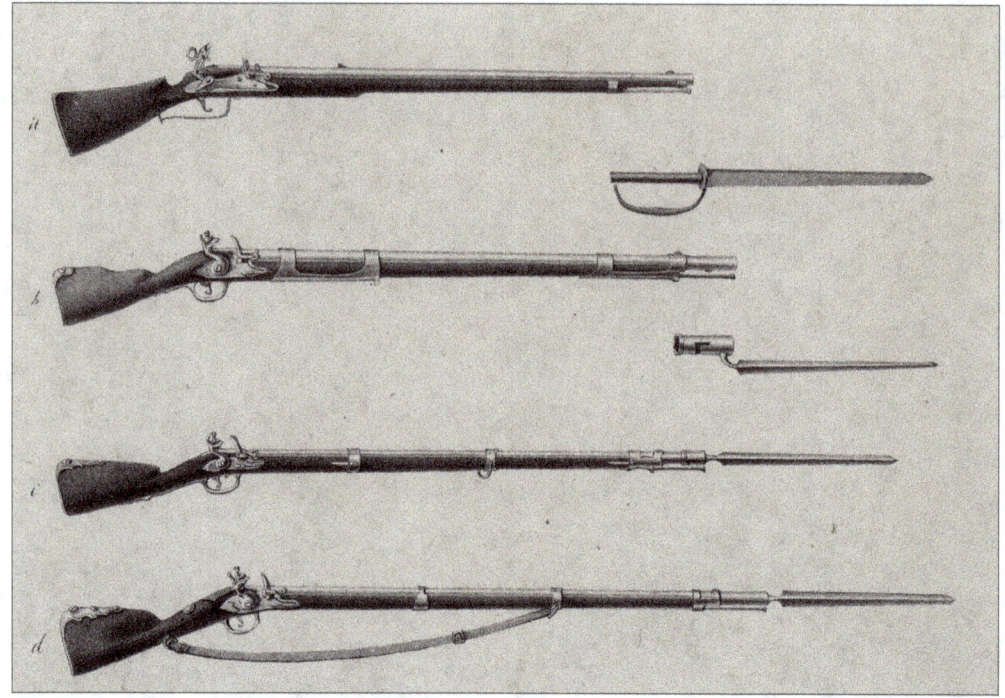

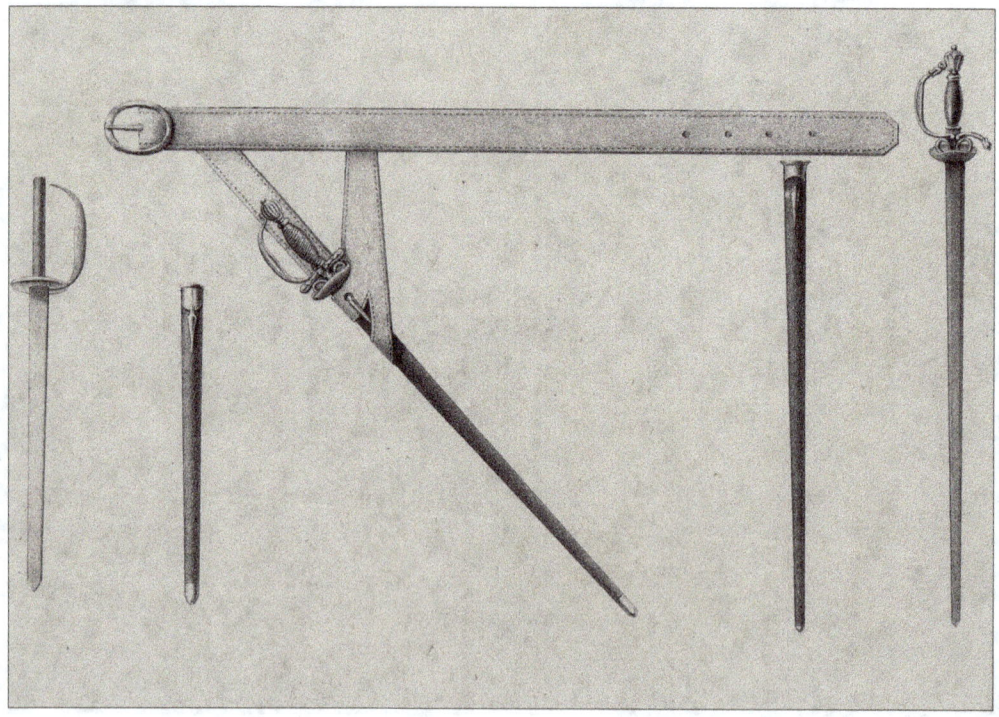

Muskets of: a) 1701, b) 1710, c) 1717 and d) 1723 years - Swords and Port epée, from 1700 to 1732.

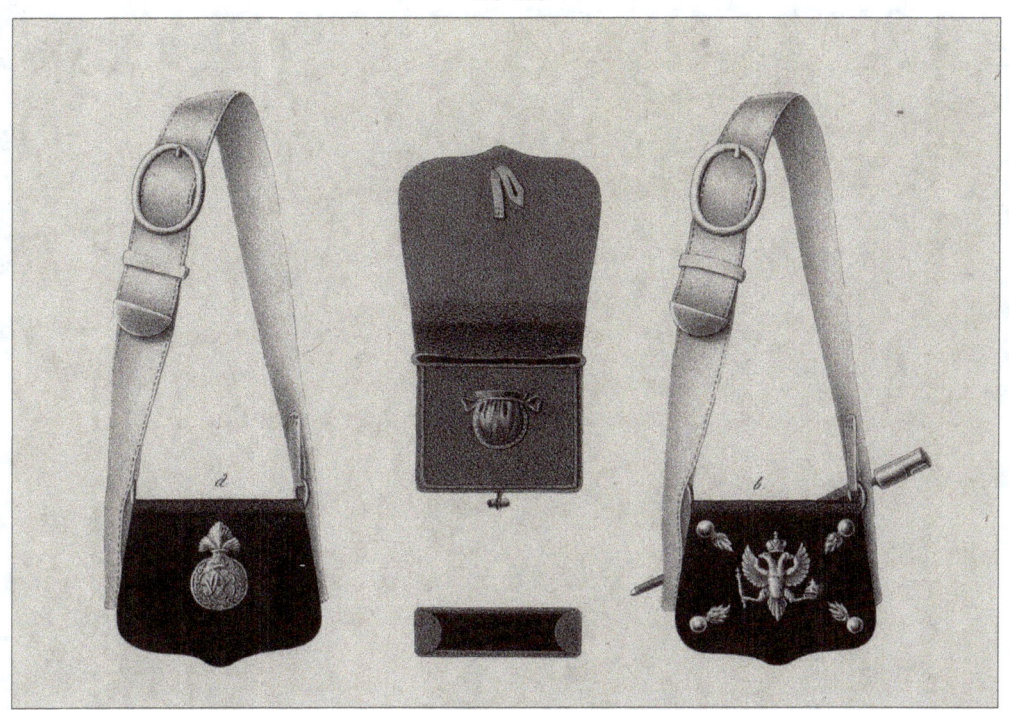

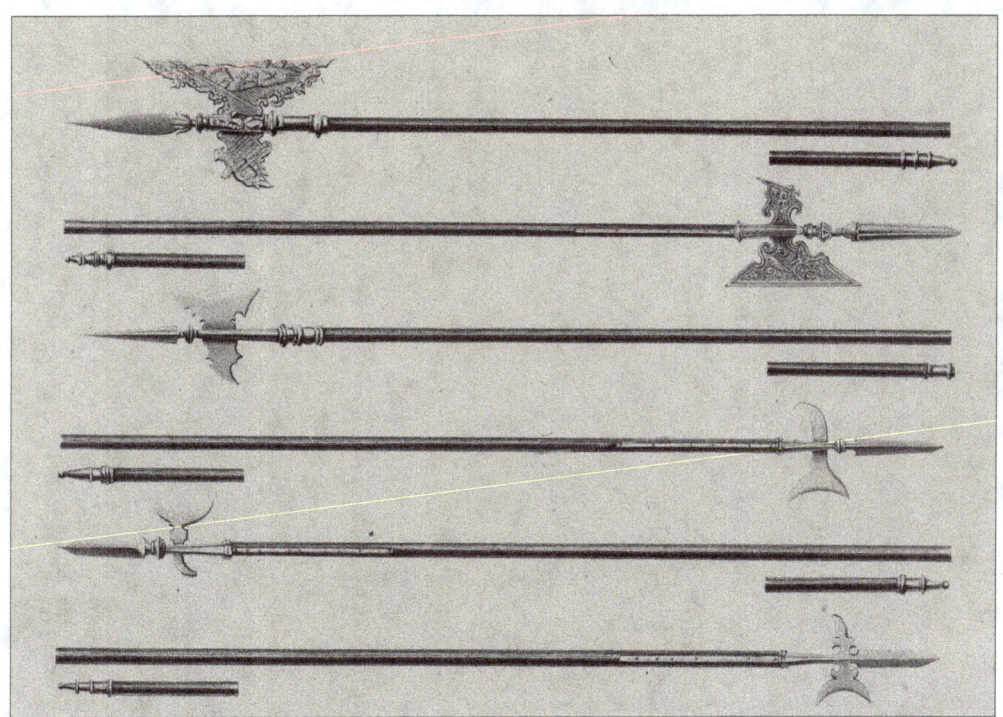

Infantry cartridge pouch, from 1700 to 1732. - Sergeant, Captain and Fourier Halberds, from 1700 to 1732.

Captain, corporal, sergeant and fourier L.-G. Preobrazhensky regiment, from 1700 to 1720.

NCO and Officer L.-G. Preobrazhensky regiment, from 1700 to 1732.

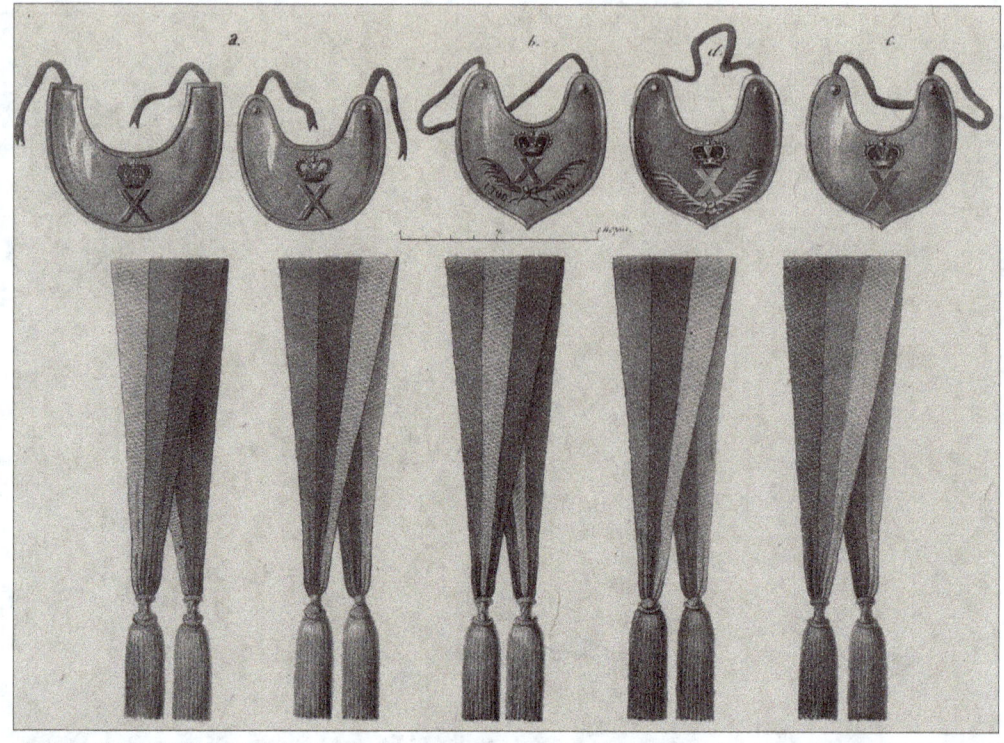

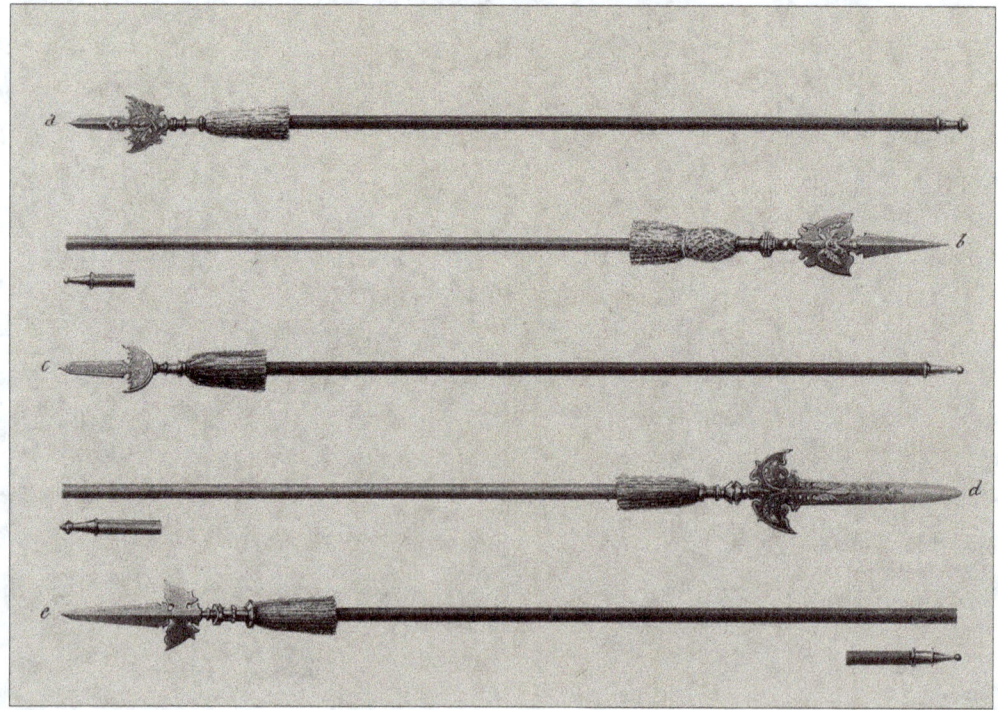

Officers' Signs, Aubert and Staff Officer Scarves, from 1700 to 1732. Ober and Staff Officers - Partisan weapons from 1700 to 1732.

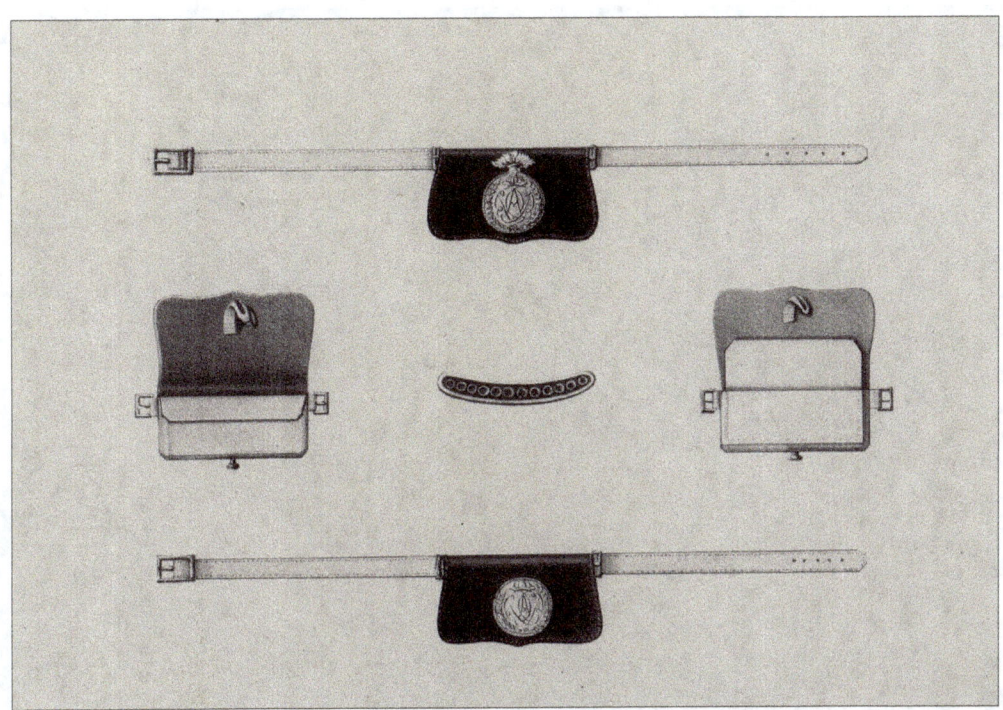

Grenadier, Pikeman and Dragoons cartridge pouch, from 1700 to 1732. - A pikeman spear and pikeman and dragoon pistols from 1700 to 1732.

Grenadier of L.-G. Preobrazhensky regiment, from 1700 to 1732.

Shakpa of Guards Grenadiers, from 1705 to 1732 year.

Shakpa og Guards Grenadier Officers, from 1705 to 1732.

NCO L.-G. Preobrazhensky regiment, from 1700 to 1732. The view depicts the house of Peter the Great, in the Catherine's Garden, in Reval.

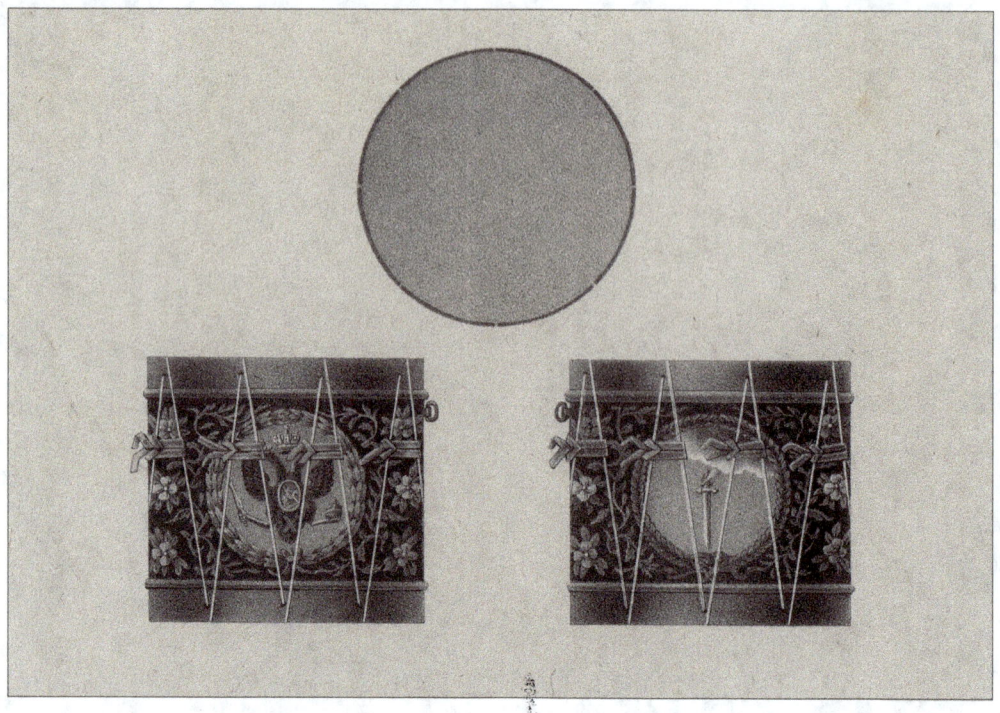

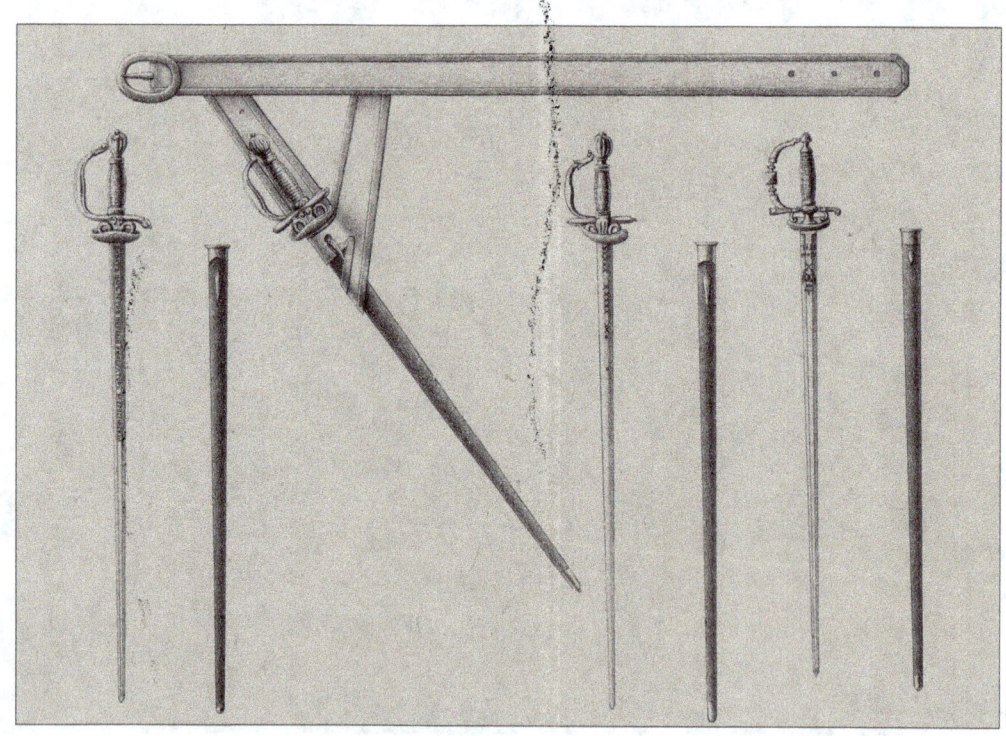

Drumm of L.-G. Preobrazhensky regiment, from 1700 to 1720-th year. - Swords of the Army and Garrison Officers, from 1700 to 1732.

Standardearer of L.-G. Preobrazhensky regiment, from 1700 to 1720.

Drummer L.-G. Preobrazhensky regiment, from 1700 to 1720-th year.

Fusilier of L.-G. Semenovsky regiment, from 1700 to 1720.

Officer of L.-G. Semenovsky regiment, from 1700 to 1720. The view depicts Ivangorod Castle, with part of the fortress of Narva.

Fusilier Infantry regiments, from 1700 to 1720.

Kartuzy caps Army Infantry and Cavalry, from 1700 to 1720.

Sergeant of the Inf. Reg. from 1700 to 1720. The view depicts the Fortress Marienburg, in Livonia, conquered by the Russian troops in 1702.

Grenadier Infantry Regiment, in 1700 to 1732.

Grenadier Shapka Army and Garrison regiments, from 1700 to 1732.

Officer of the Infantry Regiment, from 1700 to 1732. The view depicts the time part of the St. Petersburg side, with the Cathedral of the Holy Trinity, the living-room, the fairy-tale colleges and the house that served the residence of Peter the Great, at the base of the SP-burg.

Fusilier Dragoon Regiment, from 1700 to 1720.

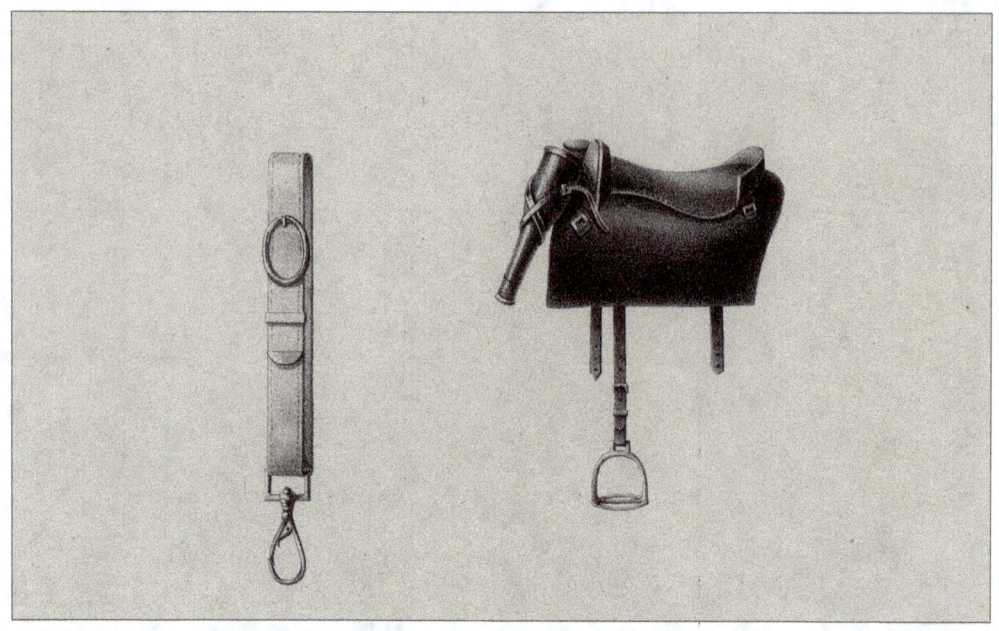

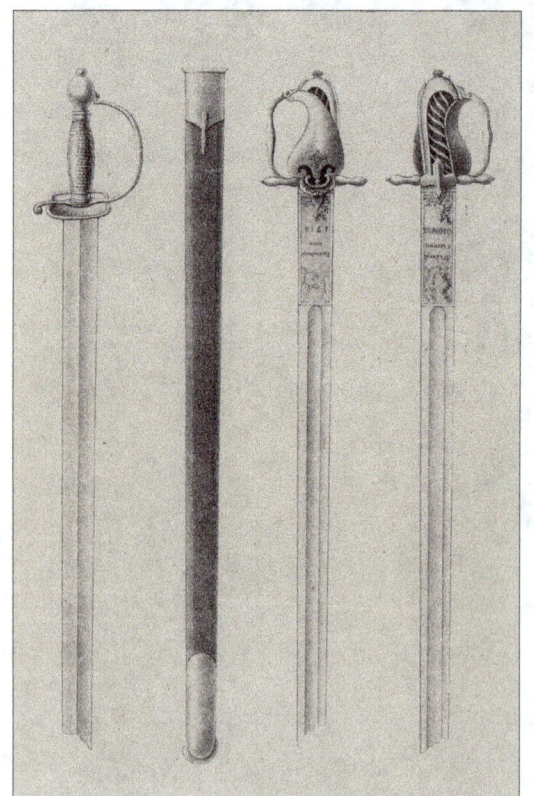
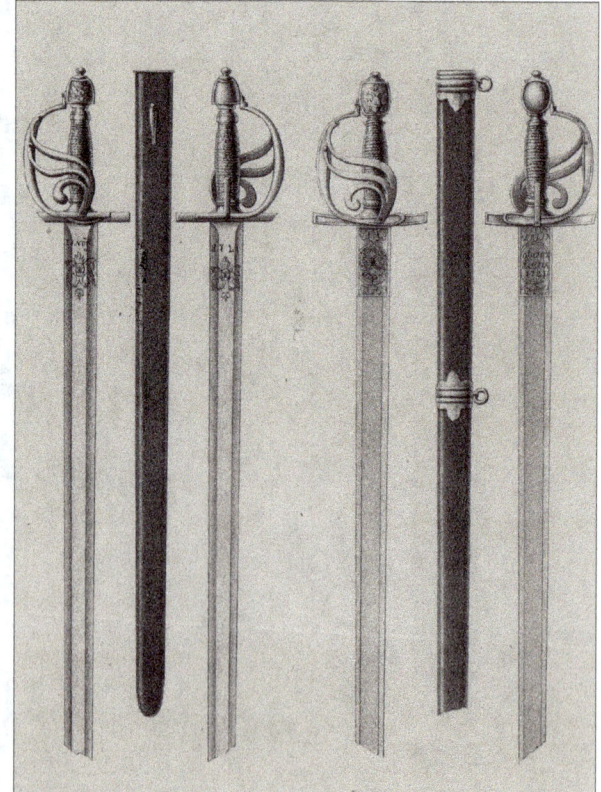

Dragoons' Palashas, from 1700 to 1732. - Dragoons' sling with a hook and a saddle with an elm, from 1700 to 1732.

Officer of the Dragoon Regiment, from 1700 to 1732. The view depicts the time the fortress of Yamburg.

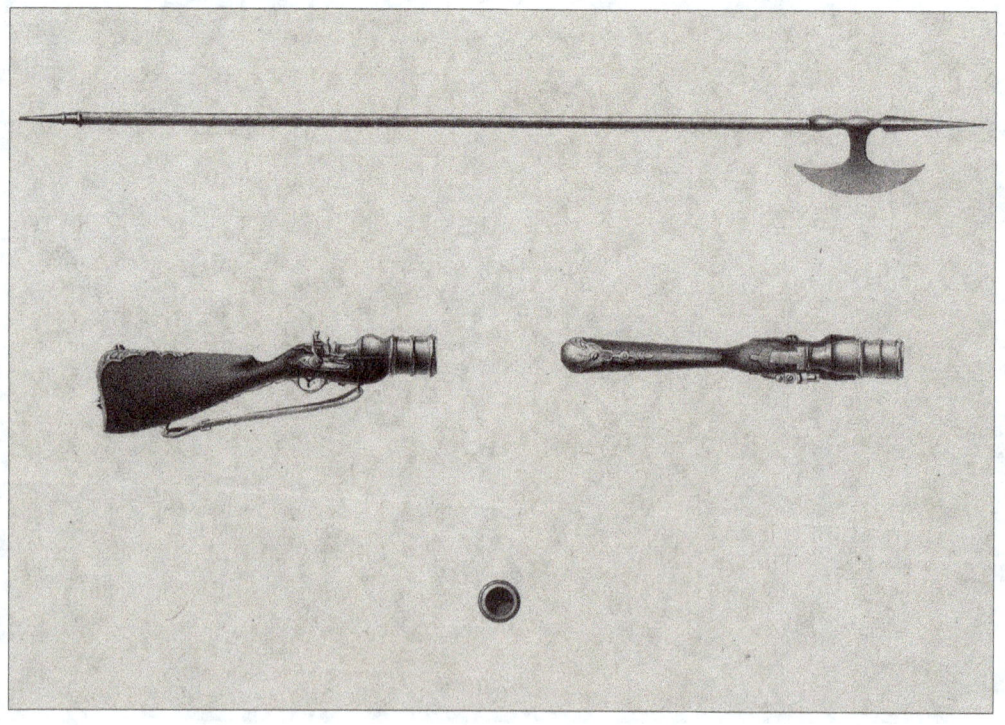

The Dragoon Timpani, from 1700 to 1732, from 1712 to 1732. - Halberd and hand mortar bombardier of the Artillery Reg., from 1712 to 1732.

Officer, bombardier and fusilier of the Artillery Reg. from 1712 to 1720. The view depicts part of the Kremlin wall and Arsenal, in Moscow.

Sergeant and Fusilier L.-G. Preobrazhensky regiment, from 1720 to 1732.

Fusilier L.-G. Semenovsky regiment, from 1720 to 1732.

Officer L.-G. Semenovsky regiment, from 1720 to 1732.

Fusilier Infantry of the Army Regiment, from 1720 to 1732.

Fusilier of the Army Dragoon Regiment, from 1720 to 1732. The view depicts the time part of St. St. Petersburg Admiralty, the Church of St. Isaac of Dalmatia and the house of Prince Menshikov.

Infantry Garrison Regiments, from 1720 to 1732. In the service and working clothes.

Fusilier Dragoon Garrison Regiment, from 1720 to 1732.

NCO of the Artillery Regiment, from 1720 to 1728.

Ukrainian land militia, from 1713 to 1736 year.

Cavalry Guards in 1724.

Little Russian Cossacks in the beginning of the XVIII century, Kazak registered or elected.

Little Russian Cossacks in the beginning of the XVIII century, Cossack.

Little Russian Cossacks in the beginning of the XVIII century, Cossack NCO.

Little Russian Cossacks in the beginning of the XVIII century, Colonel.

Zaporozhets in the XVIII century.

Cavalry garde Timpani, 1724 and from 1726 to 1731. - The banner of L.-G. Preobrazhensky regiment, 1700 year.

The banner of L.-G. Preobrazhensky regiment, 1700 year. - The banner of L.-G. Semenovsky regiment, in 1701.

The banner of L.-G. Preobrazhensky regiment, 1707 year. - The banner of L.-G. Semenovsky regiment, in 1706.

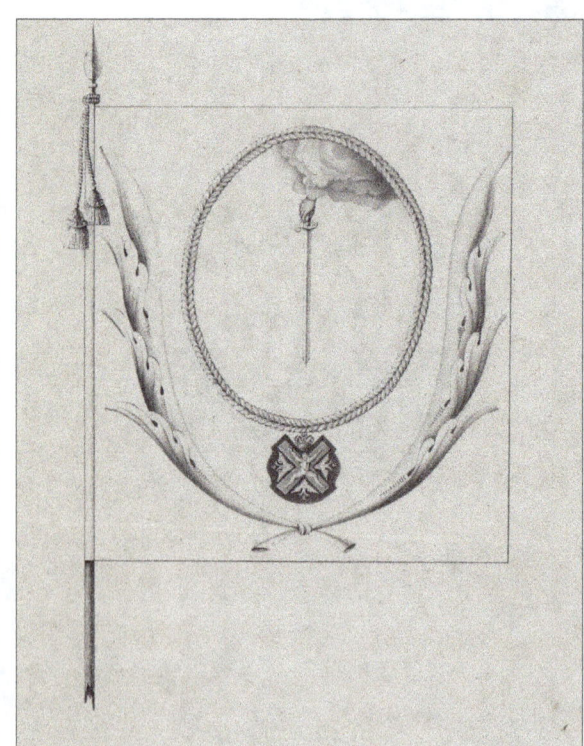

Banner of the reg. of L.-G. Preobrazhensky and Semenovsky on the 25th of February, 1711. - 230 Banner of the Army Regiments, 1700-1727.

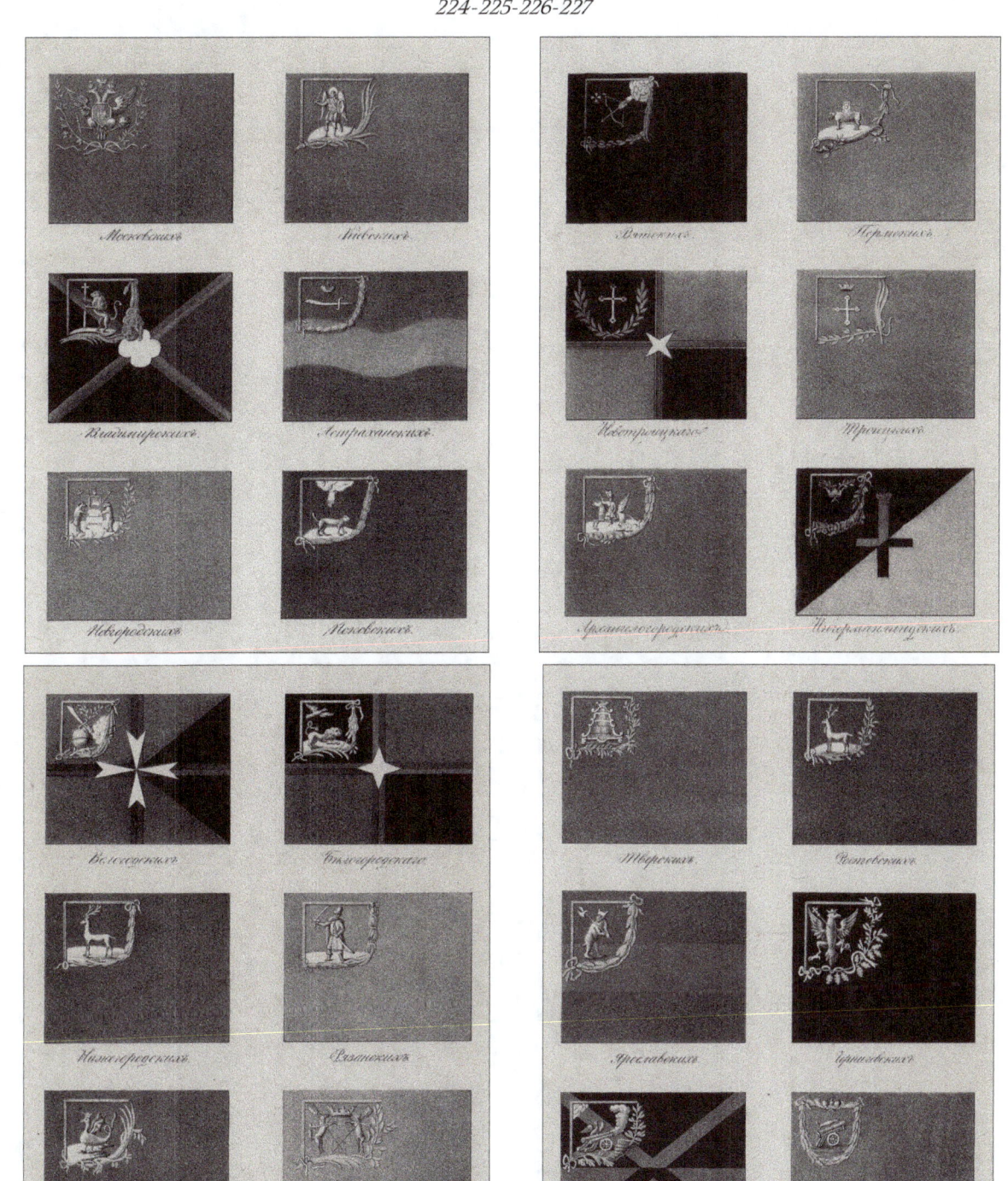

Banner of the Army Regiments, 1700-1727.

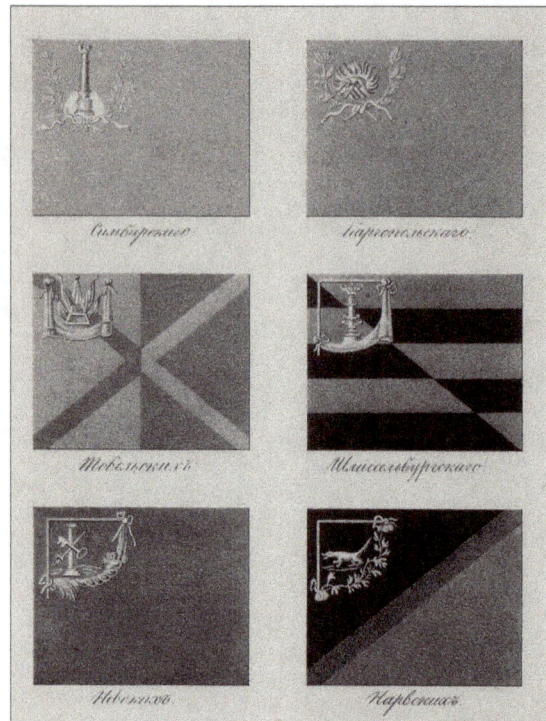

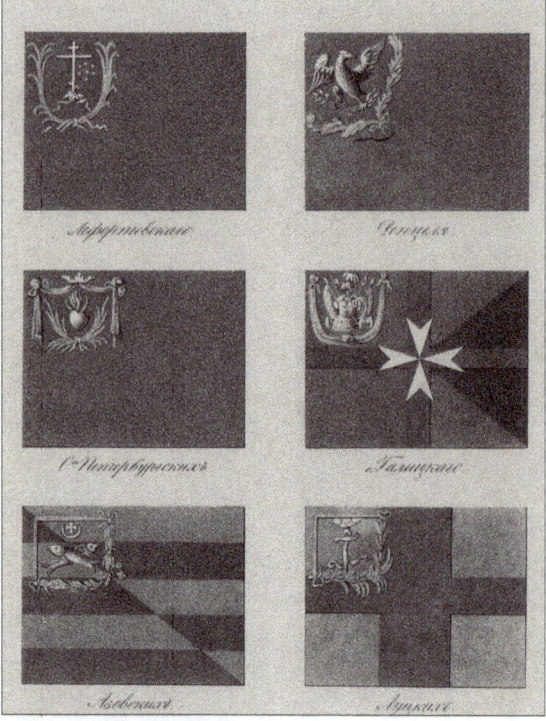

Banner of the Army Regiments, 1700-1727.

Soldat and officer of the Leib-Regiment, from 1727 to 1730.

The banner of L.-G. Preobrazhensky regiment, 1725-1727. - The flag of the Leib-Regiment of 1726 - Banner of the Army Regiment, 1727.

Fusilier of the Artillery Regiment, from 1728 to 1732.

Corporal, sergeant and officer of the Artillery Regiment, from 1728 to 1732.

Musician of the Artillery Regiment, from 1728 to 1732.

Officer and Ingenner of the Artillery Regiment, from 1728 to 1732. The view depicts the time a foundry barn, on the banks of the Neva River, in St. Petersburg, in place of the present foundry tower.

Worker soldier of the Artillery Regiment, from 1728 to 1732.

Profos Artillery Regiment, from 1728 to 1732 year.

Conductor, men and worker of the Artillery Regiment, from 1728 to 1732.

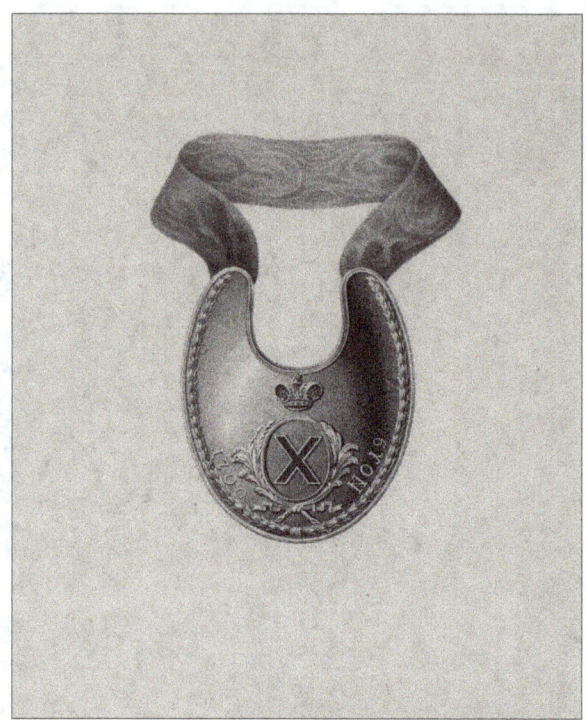

NCO Sign of L.-G. Preobrazhensky and Semenovsky regiments, 1727-1732. - The banner of L.-G. Preobrazhensky regiment, 1727-1730.

Banner of the 1st Moscow Reg. 1727. The White Flag of the Army Regiment, which did not have its own coat of arms, November 11, 1727. The Banner of the Army Regiment, which had its own coat of arms, November 11, 1727. The Colored Flag of the Army Regiment, which did not have its coat of arms, November 11, 1727.

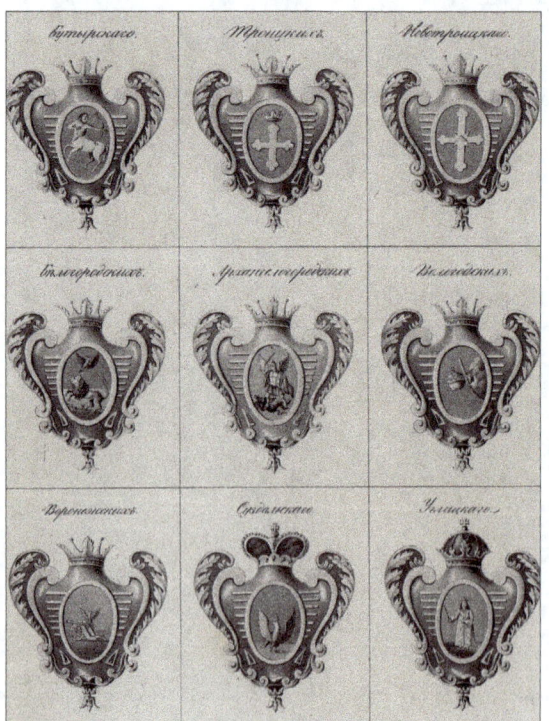

The arms of the Army and Garrison regiments, approved on March 8, 1730.

The arms of the Army and Garrison regiments, approved on March 8, 1730.

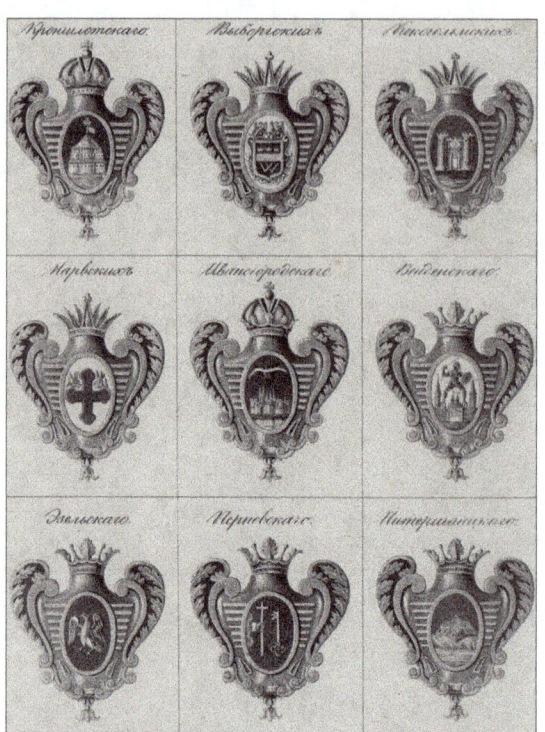

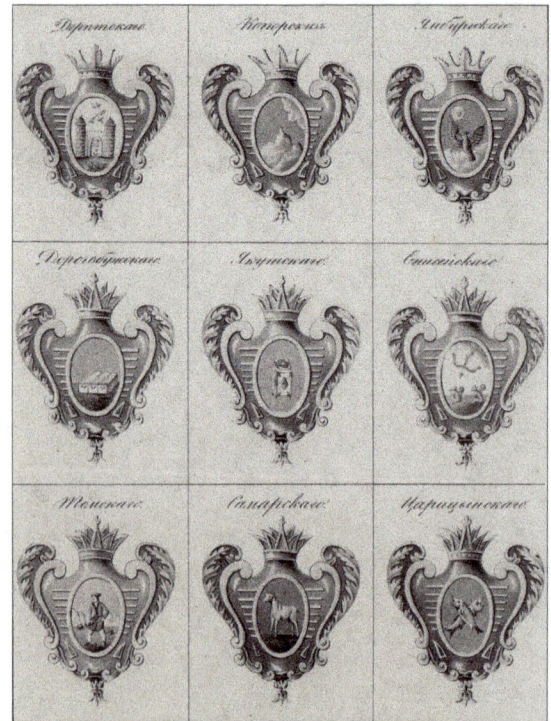

The arms of the Army and Garrison regiments, approved on March 8, 1730.

Musketeer of infantry 1732-1742

Tricorne of Musketeer of infantry 1732-1742

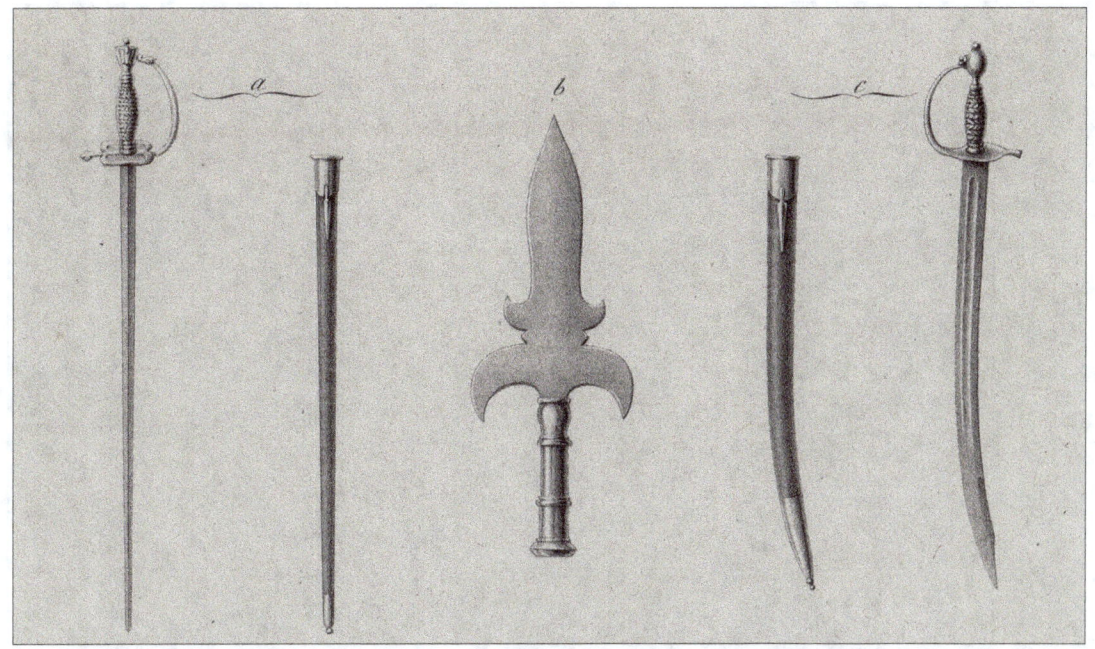

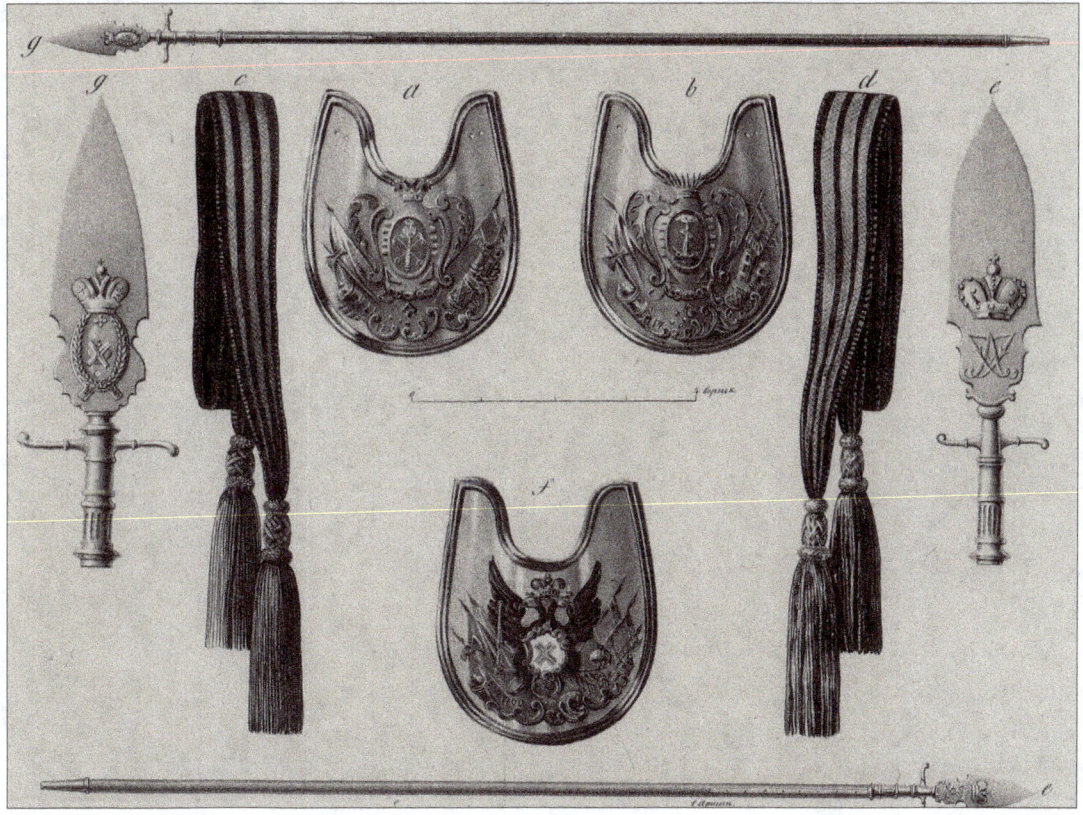

Sword and scabbard of officer from 1732 to 1742. - Sash, Partisan and gorged of officer from 1732 to 1742.

Officer of the Infantry Regiment, from 1732 to 1742. The view depicts Sukharev Tower in Moscow.

Grenadier and NCO of an army uinfantry regiment from 1732 to 1742.

Grenadier Shapka army and Garrison regiments from 1732 to 1756 year.

Private of Dragoon Regiment, from 1732 to 1742.

Officer of the Dragoon R. from 1732 to 1742. The view depicts the time the Church of St. Isaac and the main Admiralty in the St. Petersburg.

Grenadier of the Dragoon Regiment, from 1732 to 1742.

Garrison regiments, from 1732 to 1742. In working and combat clothing. The view depicts the ruins of the castle of Ronneburg in Livonia.

Private and Officer of the Cuirassier Regiments, from 1732 to 1742

Officer and private of the Cuirassier Regiment, from 1732 to 1742.

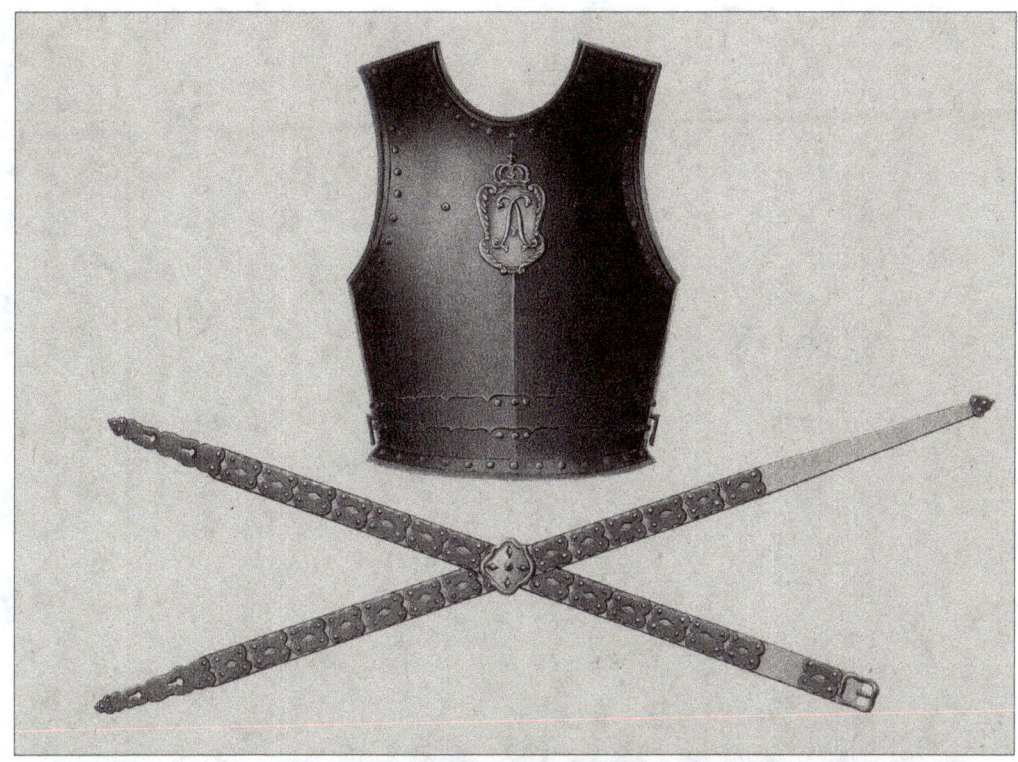

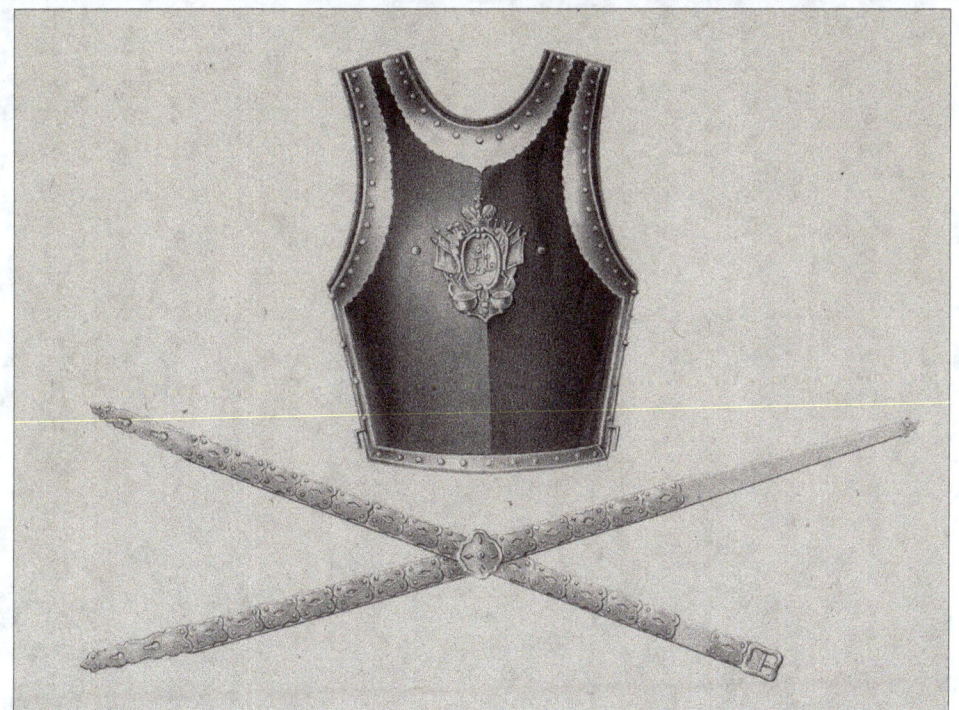

Cuirass of the lower ranks of the Cyrsir regiment, from 1732 to 1742. - Cuirass of the Officers of the Cuirassier Regiments, from 1732 to 1742.

Private and officer L.-G. Preobrazhensky Regiment, from 1732 to 1742.

Grenadier OFFICER and Grenadier L.-G. Preobrazhensky Regiment, from 1732 to 1742.

Men of the L.-G. The Semenovsky and the SL. L.-G. Izmaylovsky regiments, from 1732 to 1742.

Officer of the L.-G. The Horse Regiment, from 1731 to 1742.

Cuirass of the L.-G. The Horse Regiment, from 1732 to 1742. - Cadet Supervest, from 1732 to 1762.

Land militia, from 1736 to 1742 year.

Officers of land militia, from 1736 to 1742.

Cadets Grenadier and Fusilier, from 1732 to 1742.

Grenadier Shapka Cadet Corps, from 1735 to 1762 year.

Cadet in the Horse Carriage, from 1732 to 1742. The view depicts a house, formerly the former Prince Menshikov, when he was appointed to the Cadet Corps in 1732.

Fusilier Officer of the Cadet Corps, from 1732 to 1742.

Bunner of the Army and Garrison Infantry Reg. October 28, 1731. (The Butyrsky Regiment). - Standard of the Cuirassier Reg 1731.
The banner of L.-G. Preobrazhensky regiment, 1732-1742. - The banner of L.-G. Izmaylovsky regiment, 1731 year.

Monogrammed images of the name of Empress Anna Joannovna, installed for the banners. - The flag of the Fusilier mouth of the Cadet Corps, 1732-1760. - Standard of the Horse Company of the Cadet Corps, 1732.

SOLDIERS, WEAPONS & UNIFORMS ALREADY PUBLISHED
(SOME TITLES)

UNIFORMS OF RUSSIAN ARMY IN THE ERA OF ANCIENT TZAR
FROM THE REIGN OF VASILI IV TO MICHAEL I, ALEXIS, FEODOR III DURING THE XVII th CENTURY
A.V.VISKOVATOV — LUCA STEFANO CRISTINI
SWU-600-004

UNIFORMS OF RUSSIAN ARMY OF PETER I THE GREAT
FROM THE REIGN OF PETER I TO CATHERINE I, PEER II, ANNA AND IVAN VI. 1682-1741
A.V.VISKOVATOV — LUCA STEFANO CRISTINI
SWU-700-006

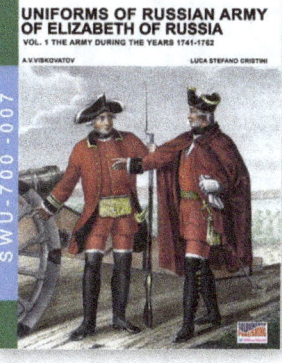

UNIFORMS OF RUSSIAN ARMY OF ELIZABETH OF RUSSIA
VOL. 1 THE ARMY DURING THE YEARS 1741-1762
A.V.VISKOVATOV — LUCA STEFANO CRISTINI
SWU-700-007

UNIFORMS OF RUSSIAN ARMY OF ELIZABETH OF RUSSIA
VOL. 2 THE ARMY DURING THE YEARS 1741-1762
A.V.VISKOVATOV — LUCA STEFANO CRISTINI
SWU-700-008

UNIFORMS OF RUSSIAN ARMY IN THE XVIII CENTURY VOL. 1
UNDER THE REIGN OF CATHERINE II EMPRESS OF RUSSIA BETWEEN 1762 AND 1796
A.V.VISKOVATOV — LUCA STEFANO CRISTINI
SWU-700-005

UNIFORMS OF RUSSIAN ARMY IN THE XVIII CENTURY VOL. 2
UNDER THE REIGN OF CATHERINE II EMPRESS OF RUSSIA BETWEEN 1762 AND 1796
A.V.VISKOVATOV — LUCA STEFANO CRISTINI
SWU-700-009

UNIFORMS OF RUSSIAN ARMY IN THE XVIII CENTURY VOL. 3
UNDER THE REIGN OF CATHERINE II EMPRESS OF RUSSIA BETWEEN 1762 AND 1796
A.V.VISKOVATOV — LUCA STEFANO CRISTINI
SWU-700-010

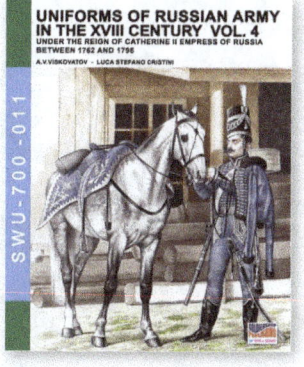

UNIFORMS OF RUSSIAN ARMY IN THE XVIII CENTURY VOL. 4
UNDER THE REIGN OF CATHERINE II EMPRESS OF RUSSIA BETWEEN 1762 AND 1796
A.V.VISKOVATOV — LUCA STEFANO CRISTINI
SWU-700-011

BRITISH ARMY UNIFORMS IN 1742
IN THE ART OF JOHN PINE
SWU-700-001

PRUSSIAN & AUSTRIAN ARMY UNIFORMS IN 1742-1770
LUCA STEFANO CRISTINI
SWU-700-002

THE FRENCH ARMY OF ANCIEN RÉGIME Volume 1
IN THE ART OF FELIX PHILIPPOTEAUX
LUCA STEFANO CRISTINI
SWU-700-003

THE FRENCH ARMY OF ANCIEN RÉGIME Volume 2
IN THE ART OF FELIX PHILIPPOTEAUX
LUCA STEFANO CRISTINI
SWU-700-004

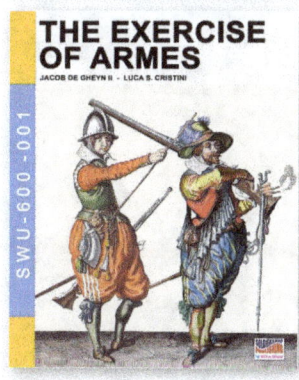

THE EXERCISE OF ARMES
JACOB DE GHEYN II — LUCA S. CRISTINI
SWU-600-001

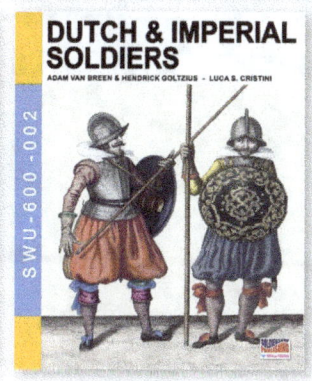

DUTCH & IMPERIAL SOLDIERS
ADAM VAN BREEN & HENDRICK GOLTZIUS — LUCA S. CRISTINI
SWU-600-002

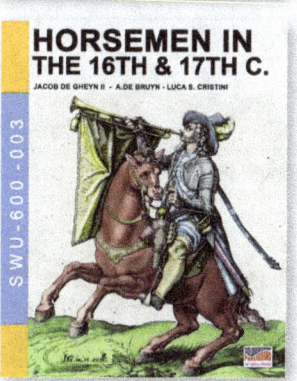

HORSEMEN IN THE 16TH & 17TH C.
JACOB DE GHEYN II — A.DE BRUYN — LUCA S. CRISTINI
SWU-600-003

IMPERIAL SOLDIERS & UNIFORMS 1640-1860
IN THE ART OF FRANZ GERASCH
LUCA S CRISTINI   Plates by FRANZ GERASCH
SWU-GEN-001